The Courage to Transition
It's Now or Never

By Dr. Robert O'Keefe Hassell

BK Royston Publishing
P. O. Box 4321
Jeffersonville, IN 47131
502-802-5385
http://www.bkroystonpublishing.com
bkroystonpublishing@gmail.com

© Copyright – 2021

All Rights Reserved. No part of this book may be reproduced, stored in a retrieval system, or transmitted by any means without the written permission of the author.

Cover Design: KeVon Pippens
Emerge Creative Group
www.emergewithkev.com

ISBN-13: 978-1-955063-18-0

King James Version **(KJV)** Public Domain

New Living Translation **(NLT)** *Holy Bible*, New Living Translation, copyright © 1996, 2004, 2015 by Tyndale House Foundation. Used by permission of Tyndale House Publishers, Inc., Carol Stream, Illinois 60188. All rights reserved.

Holman Christian Standard Bible (HCSB)
Copyright © 1999, 2000, 2002, 2003, 2009 by Holman Bible Publishers, Nashville Tennessee. All rights reserved.

Printed in the United States of America

DEDICATION

This book is dedicated to the individuals who fueled me forward in my process of transition and healing. Pastor Toby Atkins, Minister Kanitra Holmes, Minister(s) Jackie and Rueben Reynolds: I want to appreciate you in a public, permanent and memorable way. Thank you for not wavering in your support and prayers during my personal "Golgotha." What a bloody ordeal it was, but the Resurrection was beautiful. There is nothing like true victory.

You wiped my tears.
You tended my wounds.
You prayed for my full recovery.
You never wavered in your confidence in me.
You loved me through every single step.
You held me up when I could not find the strength to stand.
You understood me when others were committed to misunderstanding me.
You refused to leave my side.
I was no less your pastor, colleague, leader, or brother.

I BECAME AGAIN because you believed in the God in me.

To Archbishop Q.S. Caldwell, you are more than just my Apostolic Leader, but you are a father in the truest sense of the word. I owe it to you, your sound counsel, rebuke and prayers that kept me in position. You taught me discipline, maintained intentional oversight of my spirit, remained concerned regarding my personhood, and challenged me to handle my humanity through demonstrating grace and tact. Because of your support and reassurance, I did not forfeit the grace or the promise that was on my life. Thank you for giving me a chance and remaining unwavering in your integrity. I will never mishandle or take lightly your confidence and investment in me. What I am today is because you saw something in me that was much bigger than where I was in the moment. Forever grateful. Forever a Son.

To Bishop D.E. Williams, my forever Jurisdictional-Regional Bishop! I know you will get a kick out of that (LOL). I really look up to you. You are not just my Prelate, but a phenomenal example of what it is to "choosing honor." Your charisma, innovation and leadership are all things that I aspire to as I continue to grow in my grace. Thank you for your continual support, confidence, and encouragement.

Commendations

"God has entrusted Dr. Robert O'Keefe Hassell with a message of encouragement. This book offers a front-row seat to a difficult part of Dr. Hassell's ministry journey, but it will be an inspiration to those dealing with trying times in their own ministry. I wish I had this book when I started ministry twenty-one years ago. It would have saved me from a few heartbreaks. Dr. Hassell is a "spiritual physician" for our time and has done the Christian community a great service by writing this book."

---George William Whitfield, M.Div.

The Historic Wesley Temple
AME Zion Church
Akron, Ohio

Dr. Hassell's Book was very moving and inspiring. It hit some hidden pains of my past in The Ministry. I experienced some severe church hurt, as a young minister, from my former Pastor. Dr. Hassell made me feel like I did the right thing by not doing to my former Pastor what they did to me. When Dr. Hassell tells the story of David and Saul, it pulled me in. His explanation of David's Response to the bigotry of Saul helped me heal the hidden pain of my past. I fully recommend this book to anyone that needs the courage to move forward without taking revenge.

---Pastor Jeffrey Huddleston

Let God Arise Worship Center
Lebanon, Tennessee

Our most difficult pain is that which is inflicted upon us by those closest to our hearts -- and especially those closest to our souls. Dr. Robert O'Keefe Hassell has gifted us with an unflinching account of his own journey through one such soul-wounding ordeal. By sharing his testimony, Dr. Hassell gives us guidance for discerning harmful dynamics, maintaining resilience, and not only surviving, but thriving through life's trials.

--- Julie Wright, Ph.D.

Dr Robert O'Keefe Hassell's book, The Courage to Transition: It is Now or Never, is a compelling, first person account of how to transition in life and ministry. The author describes this book as a guide for persons in Ministry who long to heal from unseen spiritual wounds – who find themselves "having to wrestle with embracing the call, protecting the ministry that has been birthed inside them and then fighting to see it safely manifested."

He affirms the importance to heal from the pain inflicted by others, especially church leaders – a subject that is often kept silent. Each chapter is grounded with biblical scripture and examples that guide the reader with practical ways to stand on their integrity and the promises of God. He guides the readers with opportunities to see and understand how biblical characters handled their healing process.

Dr. Hassell shares his personal story candidly and honestly. He acknowledges the pain and disappointment he experienced. His openness affirms to the reader that they are not alone in their struggles. It also provides a template on how the reader can also heal from their pain. The reader was reminded that "when you struggle to the point of giving up - give in to Christ and never the situation."

This book is an excellent read for those who are struggling in ministry and a guide for those who walk with them in their healing process. I commend Dr. Hassell for his openness, honesty, and his amazing gift to guide others by empowering them with the Courage to Transition!

---Jewell F. Brazelton, Ph.D., MSW

Table of Contents

Dedication	iii
Commendations	vii
Letter to the Reader	xv
Chapter 1: Surviving Saul's Javelin	1
Chapter 2: Choosing Purpose over Position	37
Chapter 3: Trusting God in the In-Between	65
Chapter 4: Say What? Re-Routing Your Triggers and Reconsidering Your Responses	87
Chapter 5: Letting God Establish You Through Undisputed Evidence	113
Conclusion	151

Transitioning Without Fear: 161
"Need To Knows"
For The Next Place!

A Letter to the Reader

"The Lord Will Make a Way Somehow!"

Like a ship that's tossed and driven,
battered by an angry sea;
when the storms of life are raging,
and their fury falls on me.
I wonder what I have done,
that makes this race so hard to run;
then I say to my soul, take courage,
the Lord will make a way somehow.
(Thomas Dorsey 1899–1993)

Transition is one of those situations in life that can be full of uncertainties. Most people will avoid telling you about the rigor and pain of their transitions because many are ashamed of the "lived reality" of the experiences associated with it. People may find themselves ashamed because their transition carried sudden unexpected separation, abrupt relational shifts, collateral damage, loss and a season of defeat that seemed like it is lingering into their present. In some instances, transitions may be smooth. Other times, it may come with resistance, strife, and turmoil.

My prayers are aimed toward those in ministry, particularly those who are recovering from spiritual wounds — the things people cannot see on the surface. The pain is indescribable because it was caused by people who were intentional in harming them with an agenda, relentless in nature and unapologetic. This book is for those who were mishandled, manipulated, suffered collateral damage, and never received apology. May you find resolve, heal and move forward. It is my hope, after reading this book, that you will find the courage again to embrace your divine assignment. May you find the strength to initiate and engage the process of authentic healing that leads to wholeness. You are not what has happened to you. It is not over.

Get up! Someone is waiting on you! Rest assured, God is with you every single step of the way. Remember, with God: You are never out of options!

Victorious I Remain,

Dr. Robert O'Keefe Hassell

Chapter 1
Surviving Saul's Javelin

1 Samuel 18:6–9 (NLT) — When the victorious Israelite army was returning home after David had killed the Philistine, women from all the towns of Israel came out to meet King Saul. They sang and danced for joy with tambourines and cymbals.

This was their song: "Saul has killed his thousands, and David his ten thousands!" This made Saul very angry. "What's this?" he said. "They credit David with ten thousands and me with only thousands. Next they'll be making him their king!" So from that time on Saul kept a jealous eye on David.

The narrative of David navigating successfully through a volatile space, created by Saul, is a paramount foundation for knowing how to handle the insecurities in high-positioned leaders that expand into threats to our person, spirit, and call. Insecure leadership has been an issue in the modern church but has been a stronghold in presence for a long time. It is a subject that most people are scared to address due to the "intimidating nature and cultures" found in some churches today. More often than not, other leaders and even congregants suffer under the hands of insecure leaders. Their passions for their call and commitment to vision are crushed through the stress and duress of trying to maintain sanity, safety, and sainthood at the same time.

Insecure leaders are precarious — to themselves, their followers, and the organizations they lead — because a leadership position intensifies personal flaws. Insecure leaders exhibit a number of damaging traits: having over-sized and weak egos, being intimidated by other talented people who might overshadow them, being predisposed to flip-flop in course, or having paralysis when the situation requires making an ethical call.

> 1 Samuel 18:10–11 (NLT) — The very next day a tormenting spirit from God overwhelmed Saul, and he began to rave in his house like a madman. David was playing the harp, as he did each day. But Saul had a spear in his hand, and he suddenly hurled it at

David, intending to pin him to the wall. But David escaped him twice.

David surviving Saul's assassination attempts teaches us a profound lesson concerning how to navigate dealing with insecure leadership. Just because a leader sees God's Hand on you does not keep them from attempting to hurt you. When who you are BE-coming uncovers their personal insecurities, then you become a threat. This is why they are trying their best to kill you, kill your progress, and keep you dead. They want you to remain locked down, locked out, out of sight, and out of mind. David teaches us a tremendous lesson regarding surviving not just the javelin but choosing honor over revenge or retribution. David understands that he has been anointed to be the king, but his time has not yet come. We glean from this text by maintaining a posture of honor toward God's chosen servant, even in their "state of instability and angst." We should keep our hands clean and our hearts pure before the Lord.

Saul's intent was to kill David. There are people just like Saul on the Earth today. You have to be discerning. There are people who see the anointing on your life and that God's hand is on you, yet they are intimidated and even jealous. You may not know it outright, or you may even try to overlook it, but there is no denying that type of tension is present. However, it is only a matter of time before what is inside an individual like that will emerge in an open way. David did not strike back. He simply removed himself to a safe space. People who have purpose cannot afford to be reckless in attempting to react. In situations, even ones as unpredictable as these, it is important that you choose honor over dishonor. It is not easy to honor a person who is making every attempt to belittle, shame, embarrass, or kill your credibility. There are leaders who can see God's hand on your life. However, rather than cultivating it and aiding you in refining the anointing, they become intimidated and insecure. Their intimidation lingers and becomes ingrained into every fiber of their being and mutates in the "intent to kill" the purpose that lies on the inside of you.

David teaches us "how" to transition amid high tensions. Some transitions in ministry are relatively easy. They come with minor adjustments and the development of new norms in a stress-free way. Other times, transitions come with major resistance and extreme levels of attack, especially from leaders who do not want you to succeed outside of them. These types of ministry transitions, in some cases, are extremely difficult. David was caught in a problematic situation that possessed a level of toxicity that was threatening his life and livelihood on so many levels. Saul's inner resentment and jealous had outwardly showed up in such a way that it caused him to make two attempts on David's life. David had no choice but to remove himself from his presence.

In ministry, we are called and chosen of God. We are able to do what we can do because God has graced us for the task. There are many things that can interfere with what we have been called pursue, cultivate or grow. When we are harmed in any way, manipulated, mismanaged or mishandled by insecure leaders, we must make a choice to make a change. The change may come with separation from the leader, isolation by the former ministry's constituency, and even mistreatment. However, you must stand your ground and remain integral.

Hindrances brought out through transitioning from these types of spaces can be restrictive in nature because they have the ability to decrease our speed toward pursuing and endeavor, obstruct our focus, disrupt connections, and increase stress as we try to figure out the "what" behind "why." There are times, even if we have a passion for a thing and love the people attached to it, that we must prioritize changing the course of our direction. There is also another side of this spectrum: Dealing with insecure leaders in any environment, particularly a ministry context, is not healthy for our body, mind, or spirit. After a while, it can begin to wear on you. These types of barriers can put us in a place where we second-guess ourselves, doubt the sure calling that God has placed inside of us, and make us consider walking away from the work he has assigned to our hands while forfeiting the grace on our lives in the process.

David, in this tumultuous relationship with Saul, knew these dangers all too well and gave us a formula to combat them. Saul's attack on David was not just physical, but it was personal. Saul found himself in a place of distress and denial. He could not bear the fact that God was with David and that David was successful in every endeavor. One thing that I have discovered in life and in ministry is this: If people that oppose you cannot kill or distract you, they will resort to highly public personal attacks. I have seen leaders rally members of their congregation to their antagonistic cause and perpetuate propaganda by spinning destructive narratives to attack a person's character who then had to transition from the ministry. Anything that can be used to dismantle, twist, and disfigure a perception of an individual will be accessed to drive an agenda that is really rooted in their own shallow insecurity. There are some individuals who are highly anointed and gifted. Additionally, they have sincere and genuine hearts. In a perfect world, we would like to believe that everyone is excited for our "next." However, there are some leaders who desire to kill you in your "now" and pull out all the stops to ensure that you do not get to the next place. In my own experience, I have served a leader who behaved this way. I want you to know that you can most definitely get through it, keep your integrity intact and focus forward.

There are leaders who will applaud and push you forward as long as you are a benefit to them. When you refuse to succumb to their unfit leadership, toxicity, and manipulative motives, they do their level best to dismantle you. These leaders seek to shut doors, kill opportunities, and cripple your pursuits and ministry in both public and private. Nothing is off limits in their eyes. They figure, in their minds, if they made you, then they can destroy you. Know that they cannot do this at all. They do not possess that much power or influence. The only influence they have is within their limited location and area. The world is much bigger than all of that.

To add another layer of intensity, the "Saul-like" leaders who seek contest against your character often describe your efforts as having subversive motives. They conclude that these kinds of accusations would sway the outsider's interpretations of anything that you do and cause people to scrutinize even the sincerest of actions. We live in a time period where church culture is "op-ed" in nature and characteristic. People use social media platforms and the like to lay out full slates of subliminal status updates that are obviously referring to the person they have animosity toward or an issue with. Additionally, there are individuals creating private text threads and group chats wherein others become the topic of discussion. These forums lay out the latest gossip, rumors, and falsehoods hoping to vilify your character and disrupt your work. Detractors, associated with the main leader, rise up and construct false reports with no direct source that could be questioned.

If the act of sedition does not work against you in these forums, they figure that accusations against your personal life or ambitions possibly will. In the ministry world, these are the kinds of conversations that people love to share in order to dishonor, disgrace, and disrepute other leaders and their work. As a person who has experienced this firsthand, you have to know that the real purpose of all of this is to paralyze you with fear, to stop you from moving forward in any way, and dismantle anything that you are trying to build.

For those of you in ministry who are experiencing Saul-like tactics in places that you are currently serving or attempting to recover from the onslaught of consecutive pushes to stop you in any endeavor, I want to encourage you today. Having legitimate, personal success in life is so important outside of the church. Get your education and certifications, and secure an established career and stability in every area of your life. These are things that their attacks cannot take away from you. If God has anointed your life and you carry influence combined with established credibility in your field, the enemy loves to put a direct target on your back. I know that you think that everyone in the church world, friends, and supporters in your geographical area and city would want to see you succeed in your ministry endeavors. There are some that do. However, there are some leaders, like ones that I have served, who do not want you to succeed in anything. They do not want God's agenda to move you forward without them, or for you to have a fully flourishing ministry outside of them. Their intimidation will constantly show. Remember, church is only a couple of hours out of the week. Sunday morning is highly over-rated. For those people who do not have anything outside of this context, it is the apex of their achievement in gaining relevance. Do not be distracted by what things "appear to be."

Many of you may be recovering from situations like this while others of you may still be in them. If so, you may have been accused of having alternative agendas, misaligned motives, being preferential, labeled as "divisive," or even portrayed as wanting to make a name for yourself while establishing a platform. Although these situations may be filled with distress, from a personal standpoint, you must refuse to allow your anger to rule regarding the misrepresentations of who you are and not allow your need to clear your name drive your course of actions in weak moments. It is true that everyone has their weak moments and even human limitations. Nevertheless, we must choose the road of the "higher calling" to refine our discernment regarding the things that aid our progress and those that deter us from it.

David gives us a guide for responding to personal attacks: The latter part of verse 11 says, "But David escaped him twice."

As a mature individual with a future, you must relinquish your need to protect, clarify, defend, threaten suit, or take your cause to social media or any other platforms. You must realize that you cannot control what people think of you. You cannot control what people do. You cannot control what they do not hear; no matter how loud you say it. People will always dismiss you; they will forever be rude, jealous and the like. Let them. Their ability to do those things speaks volumes of them and the lesson they are yet to learn, while it says absolutely nothing about you and who you are. When an unstable leader or person in leadership treats you this way, they are giving you an opportunity. They have no high expectations of what you can bring to the table, and the element of surprise that you are able to deliver the opposite of what they expect makes people pay attention. Sometimes giving people an unexpected response can jolt them to a new reality, and they have to re-estimate you.

I want to reassure the person who feels that they are in a less than ideal position or have taken a loss publicly or privately from which it seems they will never recover. There's a cliché that says, "Lose the battle, to win the war." If you say that someone has lost the battle, but won the war it means this: Although they have been defeated in what seems to be a small conflict to outsiders and spectators, they have won a larger, more important one of which it was a part. You can lose a hundred battles, but as long as the war is not won, those battles mean nothing. Even if you have not won a single battle in the war, but you manage to keep standing longer than your opponent does, you still come out victorious. All you have to do is stay on your feet. Fantasia Barrino said it best: "Sometimes, you got to lose to win again!" If you can just maintain your posture of persistence, God will make a move!

First, David simply left the presence of Saul. He denied Saul's truth by being consistently who he really was and choosing honor. Second, he entrusted the situation to the Lord. As a result of his survival, verse 12 says, "Saul was then afraid of David, for the LORD was with David and had turned away from Saul." There was an immediate shift that Saul noticed. David simply continued on forward. However, that did not stop Saul from plotting his next move against David.

The next level was conspiracy by way of exploitation disguised as promotion.

1 Samuel 18:13–16 (NLT) —

"Finally, Saul sent him away and appointed him commander over 1,000 men, and David faithfully led his troops into battle. David continued to succeed in everything he did, for the LORD was with him. When Saul recognized this, he became even more afraid of him. But all Israel and Judah loved David because he was so successful at leading his troops into battle."

Saul's promotion of David looked like a significant opportunity, but it was not. The promotion was actually orchestrated by Saul in efforts to kill David. By Saul putting David out on the battle field, it was his intention that David would die fighting, and Saul's innocence would be maintained. However,

David did not die. In fact, he proved to be successful in every one of the military campaigns. Why? Because the Lord was with him!

One thing you must remember is that the enemy is relentless and does not stop at the place of initial attack. There is always another attempt. The first attempt was openly conducted, but Saul changed his strategy in the next attempt in hopes that his work would accomplish the desired results while leaving him with clean hands. Since these tactics were not working, David's detractor, Saul, took things to the next level.

However, David knew who he was and was confident in the God that was protecting him. David shows us that he was a leader. He refused to run from his assignment. If he had responded in reluctance, it would have contributed to the discrediting of what had already been established concerning him. David was a warrior and had defeated Goliath. David followed and honored the word of the Lord concerning Saul's position as king. David continually makes the right decisions, even in the face of threats on his life by Saul. After choosing to do what was right, God reveals Saul's conspiracy to kill David. We openly see the conspiracy and all that entailed, which is chronicled in 1 Samuel 19.

Leaders, particularly those who are self-doubting in specific areas and are intent on killing everything about you and your purpose, do not want to compromise their image when doing so. I have both seen and experienced this firsthand. Therefore, they will take to strategies that make them look innocent all the while orchestrating your demise by using other people to carry it out. The people they use are simply pawns. These types of leaders do not care about the people they are using as long as they get the job done. There are some that can be as bold as to stealthily attempt to approach you in public settings in attempts to give the surrounding observers an appearance of one thing, while actually attempting another. In my own personal experience, I had a former leader publicly attempt to convey a threat concealed as a "prayer, prophecy, or impartation" in a national convention setting. However, it is important to have people with discernment around you. Subsequently, you have to have the Holy Ghost for real and be disciplined in your demeanor. Provocation can be intense, especially when there is an impending audience. As leaders in ministry, we might not face attempts against our physical lives, but these types of threats are real. We cannot make the mistake of entering into conflict or ignoring the Lord's direction and appropriate timing for dealing with matters of this intense nature.

David continued to conquer and prevail, but Saul's intent seemingly had no end. Just know, if you are undertaking any task for the kingdom of God that advances his purpose, Satan has an endless armory of pawns and plots he will use to work against you in any way possible. David was experiencing opposition from a person who was in power. When an individual with an ulterior motive, who is in a position of authority, wants to hinder your ministry, they will stop at nothing. It is a sad thing when people feel that your demise is their come up. The leaders who do not want you to succeed will attempt to cripple your productivity by sowing discord and cutting off people that are attached to essential resources. However, that is the nature of the dog-eat-dog church environments that some of us have found ourselves in at one time or another. It is definitely a dynamic that I have encountered in my ministry experience.

Networks and connections are so important, particularly when starting an endeavor or building. Some of these leaders are very powerful and well connected to other influential people. In their attempts to stop you, they will pull a power flex by using their influence to shut doors and interfere with viable connections to discourage you from moving forward. Despite this massive scare campaign and the tactics associated, you must remain undeterred. There are also times when these same powerful people will attempt to strongarm and threaten you. These tactics are simply distractions. Depending on the nature of the distractions in play, they can place you in positions where if you engage, you can be destroyed. Keep in mind a trap does not always look like a trap, but it can be disguised as an opportunity depending on how it is presented. You cannot become so easily baited and carried away by what it appears to be on the outside. Your discernment must be in full effect and at high alert.

In some cases, there are seemingly "spiritual" people that can be sent by the leader to randomly find their way to your space to provide insight, advice, and guidance to steer you off course. Furthermore, some will plant seeds to spiral you further into a conflict or ensnare you. The litmus test of discerning the nature of that type of interaction is to check the counsel you receive against the truth of God's Word. It is when you do this, that you can determine the inconsistency with what you know about God and His word.

No matter who might be opposed to the work that you are undertaking, remember that Jesus + you = a majority! You cannot be surprised at these types of attacks. You must refuse to let fear settle in your heart. Persistence in your faith, concentration and attentiveness are the keys to finishing the work that God has assigned to your hands. The ultimate goal in completion is to glorify God and to be a blessing to those in your surrounding community. God will shift you out of that place and position you with people with an untainted pour.

In my personal experience, seeing the leader I previously served manifest behavior in the form of inappropriate harsh words and actions toward people that served was startling. Honestly, it created measures of extreme discomfort to such a degree that the morale of a portion of the leadership was low while the others fought to gain power and influence with the leader to avoid suffering the same treatment. Leaders who possess these types of behavior, in efforts to assert dominance over an individual or group, thrive on escalating issue into public hangings. These are intently enacted to poison a person's perspective against individuals. In some cases, it turns teammates against each other. Witnessing events like these, on the regular, was flabbergasting to say the least. Examples of this are—Cc'ing superiors on condemning emails in an effort to assert a measure of authority that they do not have, making public spectacles of individuals by making petty or snide remarks, and even preaching at them over the pulpit.

The justification for this type of toxic behavior is usually "this is what it takes to get results that I want." The desired results are rooted in their ability to control others by fear. Some leaders believe that exhibiting such behavior against a person will encourage others to fall in line, when in fact it has the opposite effect. As I watched some of my friends and even myself suffer public shame prior to my transition and even afterward, I saw that it only served to lower morale and create fear. A great majority sat in silence and were fearful to separate as a result of viewing this leader's approach to dealing with people who had simply had enough. In the most straightforward way, there was no perfect time to leave. I, like others, simply decided to choose my future and what God had in front of me. I underwent "due process." I knew the price I would pay even in doing it the "right way." I would rather get out, deal with whatever came with it, forge forward, and live in fulfillment. Staying in that place would have cost me my vitality, witness and character by continuing to remain covering a monster of a leader in the pulpit.

Leaders who operate from a place of fear will almost never make the best decisions for teams or organizations. It is here that I recognized that there was a power trip at play. The leader did not feel like they were in control of the situation or of the people involved and must stop at nothing to take a person down a notch to prove dominance. In their efforts to do this, they did recognize how "weak" it made them appear from those who were discerning outsiders. The leader I served tended to not reply to requests or completely ignored situations in an attempt to avoid revealing inexperience. The insecurity at play here is the fear of being exposed as ignorant. In many instances, from my perspective, I was able to clearly discern that this type of insecurity can arise when dealing with other leaders who are incredibly smart and capable. Unfortunately, I was the "smart guy." Leaders who do not feel comfortable with their expertise and their limitations will be threatened by other people who know more than they do and by situations where their lack of expertise is evident. Managing is a completely different skill than knowing. You do not have to be the expert at everything to be a great leader. You just have to know how to get results out of people in a positive way.

In this former ministry setting, there was a culture of micromanagement enacted by this leader, who took projects out of people's hands and therefore made the people who were sincerely serving feel useless at every turn. You could tell that it was driven by inflated ego (nobody can do it as well as they could) or lack of faith in other people's abilities. It is the leader who micromanages that is simply afraid to let go. The harsh truth is that if you are not competent at getting results through the skills of other people and guiding collaborative teams, you should not be a leader.

In my experience with this scenario, this type of behavior centers on fear of the unknown. For the senior leader who cannot seem to make difficult decisions, avoidance is a common reaction. It is played out in endless procrastination, reluctance to commit to bold goals, circumventing performance and avoiding letting leaders who are antivision get away with anything (even to the point of coming directly against them) because of their position and influence over them. Many times, this avoidance comes from insecurities about making course corrections along the way. Many leaders do not realize how deeply their personal insecurities play into their leadership styles.

In my experience, the leader did not recognize how habitual these behaviors had become because they were left unchecked. Not only can insecurities manifest themselves as undesirable behavior toward other leaders, but they are often embarrassingly obvious to the rest of the team—and somehow not apparent to the leader exhibiting the behavior.

Saul was a poor leader. The truth is that poor leadership behavior is all too common in the church and is typically driven by one factor: insecurity. All leaders have insecurities whether or not they admit it. However, in the case of poor leaders, insecurities often come from a personal level. Leaders with low self-awareness frequently take the impact of personal challenges and project those issues onto those who serve them, which is the ultimate outcome of not taking ownership of insecurities. I served a leader who was like this on a regular basis. My own personal Saul. Nevertheless, the experience would teach me about the value of what I possessed as a future leader and how God would grace me to transcend even the most relentless of foes I would ever face right in the church.

No one ever expects a leader or servant in the house of God to be a living nightmare. Everyone looks for leadership that is confident, collaborative and competent. The goal of any leader should be to produce other leaders with a diversity of skill sets, not a group of carbon copies. Ministry is already a complicated, yet multifaceted field of service. Working with an insecure leader frequently presents a series of challenging situations that can prove to be overwhelming. Nonetheless, there are effective ways you can deal with an insecure leader. You can maintain your posture of productivity, improve your environment and foster a productive mental space enabling you to transition to your next place with a clear conscious. You should not tolerate emotional or verbal abuse, or mistreatment of any kind. It is not healthy to submit your gifts and your person to toxic leadership and structures that cultivate dysfunctional as normal. In departing from this volatile environment, I learned the best way to handle a "Saul-like" leader is to know that their behavior is not a reflection on you or anyone else, but only of their own self-doubt. You can survive it!

Chapter 2
Choosing Purpose over Position

Purpose is something that we often do not recognize until it hits us directly in the face.

Eagles are some of the most powerful birds known to mankind. They are regal and strong and remain an iconic symbol in many cultures. But when these birds reach flying age, something very interesting happens: The mother eagle starts "stirring up the nest." With her long talons, she starts bringing up the thorns and sharp rocks, exposing them to the surface, and slowly moving away the comfortable feathers and wool from her babies' nest.

As for me, choosing to step into purpose was a reluctant decision. In former situations and ministry settings, I had mastered the concept of being #1 at being #2. I served with faithfulness, diligence, and commitment. At this particular ministry, I was in a leadership position not because I was a favorite. I simply submitted my gift to leaders, in a humble way, whom I trusted to help build a vision that would help change the lives of people. It was done in good faith and sincerity. Little did I know that this level of submission to these leaders would be a course alteration and stirring of my true purpose. When I was elevated to become an assistant pastor, I only accepted the elevation in submission to the Overseer/Father of the House at his request. I had no clue as to what transitions would eventually take place in the future or why. Only afterward and in retrospect, I was able to discern the reality of "why" and "how" I was positioned. My strategic placement was a way to show strength and stability in the swift absence and transition of the Father of the House until the other leader could regain ground and regroup.

I was only a substitute. I was never positioned to be a successor or permanent fixture. In fact, this was a common misconception by outsiders and some within the house. I never wanted it. After all, it was not my assignment. In fact, I dreaded it. I had high hopes for my professional career. Being positioned as a pastor was the furthest thing from what I wanted. I was two years post-doc and was really hitting stride. I had managed to navigate and finally find balance between ministry and my normal profession. My focus was on building that space. If I am completely honest about it, in retrospect, my positioning as an assistant pastor was maneuvered and manipulated into a "political move" by the other leader. This leader had plans to use me as leverage and even attempted to do so. Looking back on a myriad of situations, it clearly showed. However, I would not compromise my integrity to be used in that way.

First, I was placed for the purpose of sustaining credibility. I was a "trophy piece," but not an actual person in their eyes. My degrees and professional success outside of the church made me viable and well suited for the purposes they intended. The remaining leader desired to use that to their advantage. Second, my gifts could be used to build and expand in areas where very few had expertise or proven success. I had sharp intellect. I was an educator. I was a professional curriculum designer. I was a published author. I had opportunities coming right and left. I had career plans, entrepreneurial endeavors that I was pursuing, tenure-track faculty positions that were offered, and additional schooling to put me well on my way to advancing my life outside of church. However, all of that would come to a screeching halt as I was appointed to this position.

This leader had a trend of positioning people in their areas of weakness. They also had a trend of promoting people to give them a "sense of importance" to keep them attached. People, who served naively, simply served as insulation while masking the true cause of the calculated agenda of a leader who was a mastermind manipulator and conspirator. People like this acquire someone to cover their deficiencies and to push their cause while banking on their naïveté or unawareness. I discovered quickly, in so many instances, that this was being done. I was able to discern accurately that the underlying intent was plainly distorted, but unnoticeable to the naked eye. Third, it was evident that I was called to pastor and that gift showed outwardly, no matter how much I tried to hide it. On the regular, I was "watering myself down" because of the leader's insecurities, especially when charged to stand in their stead on what seemed to be a regular basis during a certain season while serving in the ministry.

The Common Misconception

Based on how I was trained and instructed in my formative years, I made it a point to really sanctify the leader in a way that screamed overkill because the insecurities within them were just that deep. I never claimed the ministry as my own. In fact, I was begging God for my next assignment because I knew going in that this was not it. Being appointed in that role was my own personal "Palm Sunday." I knew one day, sooner than later, that the Day of Crucifixion was coming. To outsiders watching this entire situation play out, I was in what appeared to be in a "favored" place. However, I was confronted by fire of perfecting that would initiate refinement to my call and mandate.

Most people thought it was major, especially considering how it was announced. I was in shock. I cried and fell to my knees. Not because I was happy or excited, but because I knew what God was about to take me through. This was my "Gethsemane moment." I did not see or view it as an opportunity. I was serving in the stead of a departed founding leader and covering a vacancy left by his absence. That, in and of itself, carried a lot of questions. I trusted God. I was counting on him to lead me through each layer of difficulty in every endeavor. It was stressful and not in a good type of way either. Being in this role was not the easiest. The sacrifice, being on call and staying prepared for almost anything, was the demand of the day. With limited insight and limited communication, developing and addressing the needs of a young congregation were mentally exhausting. A church environment that appeared to be the epitome of ministry was nothing more than layered dysfunction and a struggle against the ego of one person. This proved to be extremely trying for me in my position. Dealing with the two-faced nature of the other leaders, their secret resentment, jealousy, and the covetous nature of individuals proved to be a tedious undertaking.

Looking back, I can acknowledge that my blind side was my zeal in service. What I did not see is the fact that I served so well, even on what I considered to be my worst days. I could do almost any task instantaneously that would take others tremendous difficulty to do. My ability to execute was intimidating to some. I was your typical "Church Boy Scout," literally prepared for anything. I desired to please God, serve His people and do it well. No matter if the intent was sincere or genuine, it was an "offense" to those who were immature and unfit for the level of excellence it took to execute in this ministry. There were some onlookers who simply thought it was a spot behind a pulpit, preaching and having your name called on a regular basis. It was far from that. For me, it was a living nightmare.

Congregational care is one dynamic of ministry but carrying both the preaching and teaching weight is another thing altogether. There were so many times that I was set up to fail in the most horrible way, especially in preaching ministry. The texts that I was given were pastoral in nature. However, I was not the pastor. Nevertheless, I would seek the Lord in "how" to approach the preaching assignments. I would be given scriptural text to preach that would ultimately sink a service or be left to pick up an incomplete series that was started. Nevertheless, I would seek the Lord in "how" to approach the preaching assignments. In full transparency, because I discerned the leader's intentions, I would email entire manuscripts for the sake of integrity. I wanted what I spoke out of my mouth to be in print, so that my words could not be manipulated otherwise. This was done to deal with some of the other leaders who coveted the position that I was in and were on standby to find some opportunity to sabotage or fuel any type of tensions while the senior leader was absent from the pulpit.

God would grace me to deliver the Word, complete the task set before me, and exceed expectations. The altar would be full, and God would move in a tremendous way. People would even join the ministry. This, in turn, would only infuriate those who were intimidated and insecure. Upon the senior leader's return, they would make snide comments across the pulpit about how the church responded in worship when they did not "get with them" like they expected. Statements like, "You all were jumping and shouting like there was no tomorrow this past Sunday, but you want to sit in here quiet today." All I could do is simply shake my head. Any good leader would be grateful to see that the ministry would carry on in their absence and that God would move among the people. However, this was not the case with this leader. It was all about them. Until this day, it still is. People are simply disillusioned and ensnared by their inability to recognize that they are being preyed upon by their own unawareness of their own self-worth. This is what makes this leader so powerful.

However, most people cannot see it. There are "two faces" under one hat. Jealousy, I discovered through these experiences, especially in church, is as cruel as the grave and brings out the worst in people. People are so title driven and get high off of having an adrenaline rush from being behind a microphone in front of people, that they will do anything to maintain it.

I came to a place where I had to ask God, "What was the purpose of me being positioned like this?" After all, I was more than the position I was assigned to in church. In truth, I did not want to be "boxed in" by this position and be defined by it from the perspectives of outsiders. After all, I had worked for years to obtain a life "outside" of church. Upon experiencing the trauma from an insecure senior leader such as this, along with individuals positioned in conjunction with them, I had to make a life-changing decision. I could no longer settle in a place that was trying its best to kill me and serve a leadership structure that was built on fear, control, and manipulation of the highest type.

Surviving Friendly Fire

Ministry and the Church are two of the bloodiest battlefields that exist. You not only have to worry about enemy fire, but you have to be aware of "friendly fire" as well. As I reflect, coming into that particular ministry, there were people whose behavior signaled automatic distrust from the beginning. From the day I said, "Yes" in obedience to honoring my word, there was an unspoken envy that rested on some individuals whom I served with in leadership. It was evident, and I was very much aware. From that day forward, the secret plotting against me began. Unfortunately, backstabbing is part of human nature. But plotting against someone is also rampant in groups, organizations, and the like. Unfortunately, as long as human characteristics such as insecurity, jealousy, and competitiveness exist, there will always be someone who is out to get someone else.

As a leader, I found myself in so many difficult spaces in attempts to uphold the sentiments and vision of a leader, who in turn was angst-ridden and created this competitive atmosphere among the leadership and constituency. Quarrels of various kinds were commonplace and over the smallest things at that. The leader seemed to be extremely entertained by orchestrating chaos. The start of petty quarrels was commonplace. I never was one for fighting, particularly in church. I was almost optimistic that anything could be worked through with the right perspective and work of individuals towards a collective effort. However, before transitioning from that place and the role associated with it, there were two instances where petty fights or quarrels emerged with people who were secretly strategizing against me. I knew all along what was going on and what they were attempting to do. In knowing this, it made it so easy to avoid being easily baited into conflict. Their goal was contention. I had other leaders and even some elders take pleasure in pushing my buttons, in public forums with other clergy, in hopes of causing me to have a lapse in judgment and compromise my character. As much as I tried to ignore what they were doing, on the one hand, I honestly could not help but become annoyed. However, I refused to react or retaliate. I understood, on the other hand, that they were deliberately creating the tension to get a response. This was a huge sign that they were secretly contriving my downfall. All the roles were so extremely obvious. I also knew the limitations of my role, as well. All I simply did was inform the appropriate parties in authority. Of course, they were glanced over and never directly corrected. In my mind, although extremely difficult, I held the stance that the best response in this situation was to not give in. I refused to show that I was affected by getting physical or emotional. This leader used other people's immaturity in leadership experiences and their naïveté concerning collaborative teams to their advantage by creating a "Hunger Games"-like ministry environment.

Everything seemed like a competition although, from my end, it was not.

I was just trying to keep from failing and honor my word through keeping my commitment to God as a submitted vessel and the request of the Founding Father. It was just disturbing to observe in real time. In my designated role, I was simply trying to have my ducks in a row when it came to all that I was tasked with on a regular basis. However, there are odd things about working in leadership with people who are silently intimidated and secretly plotting against you, even more so when the leader is a part of the collusion. For instance, on many occasions, some of the other leadership behaved as if they were trying to out-do certain members of the team, make everything a competition between all of us or "cheapening it" in some way as to make it less appealing. Some leaders were not doing anything at all, except showing up on Sundays. If we were up for the same things, tasked with certain projects, and certain ones of us achieved a greater result, it was common place in that environment for others to find that hard to accept because the root of the issue was that they resented success in any endeavor except when the success was theirs.

People who plot against other people have a selfish streak. This was a common occurrence serving on the leadership team with this particular leader at the helm. These types of individuals are not team players and may take every advantage to grab credit from you. They were thinking of no one but themselves and were hard to collaborate with. This was a common experience working alongside certain members of the leadership team in this specific ministry environment. Situations often occurred where other leaders would act as if "that's not my job" if there was a task that they thought was below their position or job function. It also reflected the fact that they were not able to adapt to the shifts in tasks or priorities because, again, "it's not their job." Suffice it to say, it was easy to discern that the plotter would only care for something if it benefited them or would place them in a positive light. They were quick to grab credit too, even if someone else had done most of the work.

As a result, whenever I completed certain tasks required by my leadership role, it forced me to make it a habit to document the things and tasks I had completed. By doing things this way, if issues or allegations arose, I had the paper trail and the proof. Of course, in formal meeting settings, this made me look like an over-achiever. To those who were in leadership who were taking a lax approach to their responsibilities or negligent, they were only furthermore inclined to feel "some type of way" especially when their unproductivity was highlighted in the face of my preparedness. A genuine person, under normal conditions, would be truly happy for you even if your success highlights their failures while they still get credit for the success in accountability and saves the day. Because, at the end of it all, we are supposedly a team. Rather quickly, I realized that they cared nothing for the collective vision or goals for the house. They just wanted what they could get from being associated with this ministry leader's particular platform, which was not much at all. There were leaders at the table who were in it based on their own level of self-interest; and it definitely showed.

I made a point to have a pastor "outside" of the place in which I was serving. I recognized that the leader I was serving could not pastor me in the truest sense. This is not said in arrogance because I remained submitted even through recognizing their unfitness to lead a congregation. I am speaking to the reality of their pastoral leadership and ability. They did not possess the stable mentality, demeanor or skill to adequately pastor anyone, if I were to be quite honest. Those who battled rejection from religious environments, rebelling and raging against order were prime candidates to be swept into the cause of someone else's struggle for validity and relevance.

The violent terrain of this church environment was so layered. It appeared to be a haven of safety, but it was literally a living hell disguised in religiosity and enticement through charisma. Everyone in the church, at the time, was extremely anointed and gifted. However, many were not disciplined. Some were naïve and easily influenced. This is what made them so vulnerable to be controlled, wielded, and manipulated. However, it became the opposite of what it was originally envisioned to be when it was first founded when one person's ego became bigger than the agenda of God. "I, Me, and My" were the language of the day. It was not always like that though. There was a time when the authentic glory of God rested on a regular basis. This was due to the anointing attached to the Father of the House that was undeniably evident, yet often underestimated.

Exposing the Strategy Behind the Plot

As I journeyed forward, I recognized that a person who likes to get back at people has too much time on their hands. They gossip a lot. This proved to be a hallmark approach in observing this specific leader's methodology over a period of time. This was the primary tactic when someone separated or left. They utilized their time to gossip about other people. The leader I served specialized in infiltrating various circles of influence, using other people and attempting to get others to penetrate people's personal lives to find anything they could as leverage over an individual. This did not stop with me;

it happened with others as well. This leader had the mindset that it would be a lot easier to "slice and dice" someone when they have inside information. The information did not appear to be factual but was simply bits and pieces strung together to appear plausible in the court of public opinion. This particular leader, unlike anyone I have ever seen, "normalized" private sabotage. I learned early on to be wary and aware of what I shared with anyone by seeing other people endure the results of private sabotage. It is sad to say that you cannot even trust a leader in pastoral confidence without your issues becoming a matter of public discussion. If your guard is down, whatever you share may reach the person plotting against you, who may then use what they find out to their advantage. This is exactly what they did on a regular basis.

Being able to accept situations and circumstances for what they are and move on instead of dwelling on them is a great step in walking away from negativity and transitioning to your next. I chose me. I refused to settle or suffer under the hands of the manipulative, crafty conjuring that would cost me everything. Most people want to "skate around" the issues of dealing with the realities of the strife and struggle that come with transitioning out of a space or role. I will not. As a person who has experienced this in a multi-faceted way, I want my experience to be a guiding light for people who may find themselves in the same dynamic when it comes to making the decision to leave a place that no longer serves their best interest, both personally and spiritually. Will it be easy? Absolutely not. Will there be moments where it seems like you take tremendous credibility hits? Yes. Will you experience shifts in relationships and people leaving you in rubble? Definitely. Will you feel forsaken and alone? Yes, you will. However, if you survive "in it" and manage to get out of it, there is both a blessing and grace that awaits your life for its next chapters. It is during this time that you learn what it fully means to "rest in God," believe His promises concerning your life and desperately hold on to His Word.

Chapter 3
Trusting God in the In-Between

Unapologetically Embracing My Exodus

I considered my situation further by looking at the Exodus Narrative.

> Exodus 14:4–14 (NLT) — And once again I will harden Pharaoh's heart, and he will chase after you. I have planned this in order to display my glory through Pharaoh and his whole army. After this the Egyptians will know that I am the Lord! So the Israelites camped there as they were told.
>
> **The Egyptians Pursue Israel**
>
> When word reached the king of Egypt that the Israelites had fled, Pharaoh and his officials changed their minds. "What have we done, letting all those Israelite

slaves get away?" they asked. So Pharaoh harnessed his chariot and called up his troops. He took with him 600 of Egypt's best chariots, along with the rest of the chariots of Egypt, each with its commander. The LORD hardened the heart of Pharaoh, the king of Egypt, so he chased after the people of Israel, who had left with fists raised in defiance. The Egyptians chased after them with all the forces in Pharaoh's army—all his horses and chariots, his charioteers, and his troops. The Egyptians caught up with the people of Israel as they were camped beside the shore near Pi-hahiroth, across from Baal-zephon.

As Pharaoh approached, the people of Israel looked up and panicked when they saw the Egyptians overtaking them. They cried out to the LORD, and they said to Moses, "Why did you bring us out here to die in the wilderness? Weren't there enough graves for us in Egypt? What have you done to us? Why did you make us leave Egypt? Didn't we tell you this would happen while we were still in Egypt? We said, 'Leave us alone! Let us be slaves to the Egyptians. It's better to be a slave in Egypt than a corpse in the wilderness!'"

But Moses told the people, "Don't be afraid. Just stand still and watch the Lord rescue you today. The Egyptians you see today will never be seen again. The Lord himself will fight for you. Just stay calm."

In the Exodus Narrative, Pharaoh was not too happy about the Children of Israel leaving Egypt. Pharaoh thinks, "The Israelites are wandering around the land in confusion and hemmed in by the desert." In other words, they have lost their way. He knows their supplies are limited and that he might have a chance to round them up and bring them back. In order to bring things to a head, the Lord "will harden Pharaoh's heart, and he will pursue them." Some people might argue that this is entrapment at its worst. However, we already know about Pharaoh's proclivities toward the Israelites, and any "hardening" at this point is substantively allowing Pharaoh's basic tendencies to emerge. As has been stated over and over, the real goal of this final battle is that the Lord "will gain glory for himself through Pharaoh and all his army, and the Egyptians will know that He is the Lord." This seems contrary to Pharaoh having previously ordered them to get out of the country. Perhaps he really did think they would go for a three-day worship ceremony in the wilderness. But reality has dawned, and Pharaoh suddenly realizes they have truly left. The majority of his workforce has marched out of the country. It is important to note that Pharaoh had already been gathering his forces before the hardening of his heart is mentioned.

There are leaders in the church who are just like Pharaoh. I experienced my own Exodus narrative. The Pharaoh-like leader I previously served was not going to take my exit lightly and refused to let me go. They were determined to not let me go without a fight. I lived every single moment. I sat in the audience, being supposedly "sat down" with all the other pastoral leaders as a flex of corrective discipline after a confrontational staff meeting and layered disagreement. On the other hand, it was a deceptive pretext because the other pastoral leaders maintained their regular seats while another leader and I obeyed what was articulated. This act by the leader was really a control move. I endured being preached at and about over a pulpit, but I remained in control.

As hurtful as it was, I knew that the enemy was adamant about crushing my confidence, killing my influence and assassinating my future. After it had become unbearable, I prayed. The Lord answered my prayer by taking me away on various ministry assignments. The leader's agenda was an attempt to discredit me in front of the people, to show that they had the ultimate power, and to "get their church back." It never was my church, so I could not take what did not belong to me. Actually, it is God's church. However, that fact is irrelevant from their point of view. Leading people in the manner that they have continued to do is for the purpose of providing them their only real source of relevance.

In those moments, I knew that I had a choice. A choice to remain serving in a man-made appointment for someone else's benefit that brought about mental anguish, stress, and layered contention or to step out into an unknown purpose not yet realized. After undergoing due process, under the advice of spiritual counsel, I received my clearance to transition from that ministry. Getting the official release from my counsel and covering was life-changing for me. In the back of my mind, I knew that it was only the beginning of what I would face. Believe me, it was far from over. All I had was the Lord. All I could trust was His word. It would be foolish of me to even consider looking back or even looking to people whom I thought I could trust or who would even care to know the real reason "why" concerning my abrupt departure. I knew full well that all of the people who had been connected to this leader would be rallied in and forced to profess unwavering allegiance. I knew there would be every effort to paint and distort the image of every single selfless contribution and ministry effort I made during my tenure all because of one person's fragile ego. All of this would be done in efforts to appear to show the strength and continuity of their leadership, when it was really the beginnings of a continuous act of desperation that would turn into a "revolving door" of a ministry. It is important to understand that when dealing with leaders of this nature, they are unyielding in their pursuits even if it means their own demise.

Even after leaving the "right way," there was an intense level of anger displayed by this leader. The beginning displays of revenge and retribution were openly manifested. This behavior would not only continue in my moment of departure, but intensify for over two years after my initial transition. The strategy of this leader was to dismantle my entire life and prevent me from working in ministry ever again. These ploys would continue even into my journey as an Establishmentarian and Founding pastor. However, no matter what was done or said, I left with peace in my heart and I refused to turn back. I chose purpose. I chose myself. I chose a call that was given to me by God.

I walked out with my dignity, value, competence, and skill. It was something that could not be taken away. It was a valued asset as long as it was in the possession of a leader with a Pharaoh-like mentality, but it was deemed a danger and a threat if released into a place of true freedom. The Lord kept his promise to me just as He did to the Children of Israel. I recognize that this "Pharaoh personified" type of leader was merely a player in God's greater plan. I had the courage to walk away. I crossed my Red Sea and my Pharaoh was consumed.

I departed the ministry without a second thought or the slightest hesitation. There was nothing that could be said or done that could rationalize me staying in that type of environment. I had experienced enough. I was Dr. Robert O'Keefe Hassell when I entered. I was Dr. Robert O'Keefe Hassell when I exited. The position that I served in, contrary to outside perception, did not "make me" and it surely was not going to break me. I had power. I had something that man could not take away. I had influence and credibility that was undeniable, substantiated, and proven. This is the fact that the leader hated and still resents to this day. This leader's strategy was to use positions to provide a sense of affirmation for individuals who really had low self-value of themselves while underhandedly securing them to be used for personal causes related to whatever agenda they were trying to push. They had been able to destroy everyone else who had left. I stood up for myself as a man, professional and a leader. What I had become, all that I had created, and my gifts that flourished were a result of God's immeasurable grace on my life.

Although I knew the tactics that would be enacted against me as a result of my decision to leave, and even carried out against those who were associated with me or with whom I had relationship, I could not be scared or influenced by threats, social isolation, or anything else. I chose me because I was better than that. I chose purpose over a position even though I knew it would bring an intense level of warfare. I was confident that God would be bigger than what the leader would attempt against me out of retribution. I knew that there were a lot of things that could possibly happen. I also knew the schemes, maneuvers, plots, and social stigma that may come my way as a result of my choosing purpose.

    I want the reader to know that choosing to walk fully in purpose will be the best thing you ever do for yourself and for your life. It may hurt to separate, but there is safety in separation. Choosing purpose will lead to fulfillment beyond anything that you have ever known. It will give you the opportunity to find your form, fit, and tribe where you belong. God will make sure of it. However, once you choose purpose, there is no turning back. Choosing purpose over a position is going to require you to undergo separation. This type of separation will not be just from institutions or organizations, but social splits from people you consider to be friends or even closer. Sometimes separation is required for your survival. Many of us cannot endure the pain of separation.

In certain environments, we find stability, build foundations, make friends that become more like family. We cannot fathom being disconnected from those things or that there would come a day that they would all be gone. However, some of us remain stifled because we cannot see beyond our intense desire to stay connected. We fail to recognize this: There are some places where you have built your life that can no longer sustain your life. All of this may have been part of your past and present. However, there is no place for it in your future. This demands a relocation. There are so many of us that have continued in our connectivity to places and people who can no longer sustain life. We are not naïve to the fact that these things have proven to be unproductive and unfruitful. You, your purpose, and the call on your life are living on life support because you refuse to let go of everything that is trying its best to hold you back.

People do not like the word "separation". In fact, they fear it. Separation requires that we must relinquish, end, or disconnect from something. We get in our feelings when people "shift," not knowing that it is God doing the shifting to save us! We have separation anxiety, which is when someone is afraid of being separated from a particular person, persons, or place. While many people associate separation anxiety with children, adults can experience the condition as well. This is why many individuals are still stuck, still settling for less than they deserve, making justifications for toxic people who are harming them and slowly succumbing to situations that were not ordained for their lives. They are constantly complaining and conversing about their disappointment to others, yet they do not realize that their reluctance to disconnect is what keeps them in this destructive cycle. The question is not: Is there really a way out? The question is: Do you really want to get out?

Unusual distress about being separated, heightened fear, and excessive worry of being alone or excluded have caused so many of us to remain in situations by not making a choice for a duration of time; we waited on the "perfect moment" to make an exit from places we should have left years ago. This is done in hopes that our departure will not cause an uproar or any drama. We know that some people are so insecure and bent on intentionally being destructive that they will stop at nothing. Their ultimate goal is to hurt, hinder, or discredit personhood, professional credibility, and ministry.

Looking back will delay your deliverance in the present! Your deliverance in the present will determine your path to the future. Abrupt shifts that come as a result of your choice to choose better will come, but they are necessary for your survival. Looking back can be deadly and cause us to experience unnecessary delays naturally and spiritually that can threaten our progress. God desires to deliver us in the present, so we can get to the future. What is deliverance? The action of being rescued or set free, liberated. If you want to move forward in your life, purpose and ministry call, you have to give up doing something. That something is "looking back." Constantly looking back to the past will hinder you from moving forward. It is hard to look forward and away from the past. There are so many awesome things to look back upon. Nevertheless, there are also problems with constantly looking back. These problems will stop your forward momentum. Even worse, they can cause you to go in a direction you do not desire.

For example, have you found yourself distracted while driving and your eyes are focused on an accident to your left? Do you remember what happened as your eyes shifted to the accident? You unconsciously began to drift toward the accident. Your hands shifted ever so slightly, and you tilted the steering wheel in the direction of the accident. Then you caught yourself and made a hard correction. Our focus is amusing, yet ironic. We are apt to go in the direction of what we focus on. So, by focusing on the past, we are taking our eyes off of our future. This is the problem with focusing on the past.

Our course of direction changes. We wander to places we do not want to go. We lose sight of the end goal. It is challenging to change our focus from the past to the future. Especially if you have been focused on the past for an extended period of time.

We have problems moving forward from situations because our mind and memories are still there. Former positions and the accomplishments, connections, friendships, bonds formed, and the like are present in the past. It is okay. We have all been there. We may still find ourselves there at times. Yet, if we want to move on, we have to alter our focus. We cannot stay focused on past hurts, regrets, or even successes. The focus has to move to what is going on right now and what you desire for your future. Shift your eyes from the past. Focus on the present and the future. Move consciously in the direction you must go under God's direction. There is a popular saying, "Don't look back: you are not going that way!"

God does not want you to reside in any place that does not bring out the best in you! He wants you to choose purpose because He has plans. Jeremiah 29:11 (KJV) — "For I know the thoughts that I think toward you, saith the LORD, thoughts of peace, and not of evil, to give you an expected end." God desires that you be in a place that cultivates, cares, and demonstrates concern in areas of growth in your life that matter the most. Despite God wanting the best for you, it all hinges upon one thing. The one thing is a simple decision. More importantly, it is a decision that you have to make.

When it comes to choosing between remaining in a position versus pursuing your purpose, choose purpose even if you disappoint people. You must fully understand that people are always going to have an opinion about you. You might be the topic of dinner table discussions, chat groups, and text threads. However, the reality is that you have to "move differently." It is not that you are better than they are or anything like that. You just want different results for your life. Do not stay in bondage for someone else's benefit. Not everyone will understand it, and the majority will disagree depending on how they are connected to the person who is in control and trying to keep you in the same place. You will never go wrong following God into the unknown because where God guides, He always provides.

Chapter 4
Say What? Re-Routing Your Triggers and Reconsidering Your Responses

We have all probably been in a situation where someone reacted in an extreme manner after having every single button pushed. It is definitely not a pretty sight under any circumstance. You also might have been in a situation where your own emotions were so formidable that it took all of your restraint not to go down that path yourself. Maybe you can think of a time when you did not control your reaction so well. Perhaps anxiety, anger, or frustration got the better of you? It happens. However, when you are in certain positions and have so many great things ahead of you, you have to consider rerouting your triggers and reconsidering your responses.

There are some leaders within those walls who build their base by thriving on the uncertainties of others. These types of people use individuals for their personal agendas against others. Most people will not say it out loud, but the people in the Church "have teeth." Every saint with a smile on their face is not so loving. Every pastor with a firm handshake and hint of cordiality is not necessarily nice in reality. Some specialize in provocation. These types of people do this because, in reality, they have nothing to lose and want you to be brought down to their level. When a person finally wakes up to the reality of who they are and refuses to accept toxic treatment, those leaders will go out of their way to "break" them in any way possible. However, you cannot fold when people provoke you. Their provocation and your subsequent response can cost you your future. These situations require you to think.

Remaining silent when you want to respond is a discipline of the highest type. When a person is trying to provoke you to act out of character, they are trying to solicit a response from you to prove that what they said about you is true. We live in a society that centers on perception. If you are aggressively defending yourself against their onslaught of accusations and negative statements, depending on your approach, you can be perceived as guilty. This is because outsiders think that if a person is not guilty, they would not bother aggressively defending themselves against accusations. I have dealt firsthand with these types of situations as a leader and as a person.

From a personal standpoint, I can say "subliminal statuses" are the worst. As naïve as people pretend to be, everyone always knows the person they are talking about. The outsiders are eagerly waiting for what is going to happen next. People, especially those in the church, thrive off of some good drama. It is really sad, if you think about it. However, the person posting the status updates simply wants to "throw off" by saying publicly, to get attention, what they would not have the courage to say to your face. People possess that level of cowardice in real life. However, that does not stop them from doing what they choose to do.

Upon my transition from a ministry, I experienced an instance where a subliminal status update was caught by a syndicated church podcast show that reports the latest gossip in the religious arena. As I watched the entire exchange live and the story attached to it, there was nothing more that I could do. My heart sunk to the depths. My phone was ringing off the hook and the text messages were endless. The most hurtful part was people who I served alongside in that particular church were commenting on the LIVE feed and telling the inquiring minds in the comments what the acronyms represented. All signs pointed, of course, to me and another individual. Everyone, particularly those from the city and surrounding areas, knew the meaning of the acronyms and the people associated with the positions. It was disheartening to say the least, but it was only the beginning of the relentless onslaught that would take place. On the flip side, I did end up increasing 5K in followers. God is really funny like that. He always brings the best out of what seems to be the worst.

When I became the leader of a new ministry and congregation, I understood the responsibility of who and what I represented. Honestly, I anticipated the warfare that would come my way. The journey in founding a ministry and leading a people was not an easy one by a long shot. By far, it was one of the most challenging and rigorous undertakings of my life. Sacrificing, birthing, building, and planting a ministry in the city, particularly a metropolitan city, taught me a lot about people.

Think of the worst things that one person could say about another. Yes, that is exactly what happened to me and others, too. If you could think it or imagine it, they said it. The most interesting thing was to hear something about yourself every single day or see it posted about in a subliminal way. However, it did not stop with just me. The people who stood with me also faced scrutiny and social isolation and were victims of these types of attacks. More importantly, the goal of the leader and those that were connected to their leadership was to "kill me," my credibility, my influence, and to ensure that I would never be able to do anything in the area of ministry or to have success. Their stance was attributed to their leader's attempt to dismantle me, as it had been done in the past to so many other people, in the hope that it would draw me back. Others had come back, but that would not be me.

This situation turned out to be an outright vendetta. To outsiders, it seemed sure to succeed against me. The leader whom I had previously served did not want my ministry or the church that we founded to thrive. Nothing was held back in efforts to destroy what the leader viewed as a threat, even in its infancy stage. Our ministry, in its first active year, weathered a level of warfare that would have killed most ministries. It was the Nehemiah 4 situation lived out in real time. Our ministry, founded out of a call to serve people, cultivate their lives holistically, and minister the transformative Gospel of Jesus Christ, was placed under siege.

The attacks on me were a mainstay for a while. Personally, I lost a lot. For me, it was extremely difficult to digest because I had sacrificed almost two years of my life and some significant opportunities to be present for this group of people. I had engaged in pastoring and teaching while being present, alert, and aware. I suffered from carrying the weight of keeping my word to the Founding Father of that ministry. It never let up. Experiencing this could have driven a person to the edge, but not me. I had to focus. My humanity took a hit though, but I trusted God. When certain individuals could no longer attack me publicly without the reasons being obvious, they rallied under a cause. It was a masterminded strategy that was planned, tactical, and intentional. Through the influence of that leader, the priority of the day was to create and spin narratives concerning my ministry to everyone possible in hopes that it would dissuade people from visiting and joining the ministry. We endured our social media pages being reported daily for almost three months resulting in our accounts being temporarily locked, but we were cleared every single time.

Through it all, the members who were discerning of what was taking place in our congregation remained steadfast by my side. They prayed for me, encouraged my heart, remained silent, stood in discipline, and continued the work. Nevertheless, it did not stop the warfare. The attacks got worse. We were in a situation similar to Exodus 1:12 (KJV) — "But the more they afflicted them, the more they multiplied and grew. And they were grieved because of the children of Israel." When they continued to see progress the ministry progressing at a rapid rate and continuing to move forward, they changed strategies. This time, the leader and their associates targeted key people with certain resources and made attempts to keep them from supporting or assisting us in any way. They did so by thinking it would cripple the ministry from functioning. I have always been one to honor ministry gifts in a substantial way concerning financial matters. However, having been a person to speak and conduct worship at small or beginning ministries, I have always been accommodating. I attempted to make postings for worship leaders, and secure stable musicians, media team and support staff, but the appeals were to no avail. I was left on "read," ghosted, or received no reply. I was locked out. For those whom we did secure in the beginning, we were charged outlandish rates for a small ministry. The most astounding part was that they would treat our ministry like a gig. People who were connected to the former leader or who associated in mutual circles were prompted to change rates to discourage us from ever getting off the ground. Honestly, I would have rather heard, "No. I don't want to do it!" or "I respectfully decline." I did not even get that at all. It was extremely hurtful.

I must be truthful as I reflect; there are some moments that I will never forget. We invited a guest worship leader and team to minister. This occurred during the pandemic, but we had all the protocols in place for a safe production. The sanctuary seats 250 people. It was more than enough space to sit socially distanced. The worship leader and the team would not even come into the sanctuary to sit for the service. They remained in the Fellowship Hall until they were called up to sing, and then returned to the Fellowship Hall immediately afterwards. During the service, you could tell that the leader and their entire team had a disposition of "Let's just get this over with." As I stood by to watch, I made up in my mind that I would never subject myself or our ministry to that type of situation ever again. It became extremely apparent that they were apprehensive about being there because of their connections to other people, as well as what they had heard about me and the ministry. People talk, and I was not naïve of that fact. It was quite obvious based on their expressions, body language, and disposition on the live feed. The funny thing was the entire "Praise and Worship" piece was muted. It was an accident, but divinely ironic.

When that did not work, the leader and members of their congregation changed strategies yet again. This time they intentionally targeted individual members who had already joined our ministry, as well as people who had recently connected. They did not stop there. They also targeted some of the people who were aspiring to join and were what you would call "dating" the church. Their conversations were intentional in making attempts to sow discord and discourage them from becoming a part of the ministry while portraying the ministry as rebellious and antagonistic against them. This was done in hopes that it would break the ministry from the inside out and cause us to dissolve altogether. Truthfully, there were some people who left. These members did not even have the courage to have a direct conversation with me, even considering that they were told up front what was happening and why it was happening. This was the hurtful part, especially after pouring and investing.

The continual blows were devastating. People whom I genuinely loved, cared, and prayed for turned away from me because they did not want their loyalty questioned. It was disappointing because I thought church was not the epicenter of our relationship. Just because I did not remain in a ministry, I was treated like an enemy. This leader and the ministry perpetuated that type of behavior as a part of their church culture — and they still do. They would see me or others and would literally run the other way to keep from speaking. Persons whom I considered to be close friends and colleagues distanced themselves from me, and many walked away acting as if they never knew me. I was scrutinized publicly and privately by individuals with whom I had served, even when they knew the "what" behind the "why." Yet their blind allegiance, actually rooted in fear, to toxic leadership made them succumb to be a part of the whole agenda. I understand, in retrospect, that they simply lacked the courage to stand for what is right. Not everyone is brave enough to go against the grain: to be bold enough to leave and never look back.

I was a person. I was a man first. The prefix in front of my name had nothing to do with it. It was not a struggle for me because I knew "who" and "what" I was. I knew I was capable, credentialed, with three legitimate degrees in tow, and highly qualified.

However, that was not the apex of my being. I was a great person. I was a great friend. I had a good heart. I loved people. Most importantly, I knew that God's hand was on my life and I was anointed to accomplish what he had set before me. When you are sure of your call and the God that has called you, there is no second-guessing it whatsoever.

People within the city knew what was going on. All eyes were on me. They knew that transition had taken place. However, the "why" behind the transition was left to be interpreted by only one side of a narrative that rapidly spread like wildfire. Some were perplexed, but others were not because they knew the ways of that leader. As I reflect, there were some venomous things said about me. To hear it and experience it through actions was enough to eat away at a person and cause them to enter a downward spiral. When a leader and a group of people repeat something over and over, most individuals will consider it to be true. Contesting it, even with genuine intent, only adds fuel to the fire. I was not going to waste time or energy focusing on any of that at all.

No matter what is thought or publicly said about you, you must learn to simply go through it. I would say that God gave me a grace to endure hardness. I will tell you, firsthand, it is not the easiest thing to bear. I appreciate it because it helped me become disciplined in my emotions, made room for people whom I really needed at the next level, allowed me to experience authentic support and love, make clarity-filled decisions, and move in a strategic way on purpose. As a leader, throughout the entirety of my transition, I said absolutely nothing. No reactions. No replies. No responses. I stood still and rested, no matter how I was treated. I did not chase down the lies. I did not try to win over people by trying to tell my side. People believe what they want to believe and who they want to believe. It does not even matter whether the facts are present. A person's allegiance will always be to the one they deem worthy of it. My stance was this: The people who knew me, knew my intent, and knew what I did. They also knew what I did not do, which was why I was receiving the type of treatment that I was getting.

As a leader, it is not easy to silently watch and endure this while remaining in control and shepherding people through it. I had to rethink my responses and consider my engagement. I represented someone and a cause that was bigger than myself. When other people's recommendations are on the line concerning you, particularly your superiors, you do not allow your behavior to be compromised to speak otherwise. I would advise someone going through a similar situation as such: "You reach the point in your life where you value your future more than a fight." When you have more years in front of you than behind you, do not let certain stuff or people bother you! Keep your focus and keep winning! I realized that my future was more important, and I was the one with more to lose in the end.

I pastored through it, remained steadfast in my stance, and served as an example of leadership to those assigned to me. I was always taught to "Sanctify the Leader in the Eyes of the People!" In spite of what was said and even those things that were intentionally done, both openly and secretly, by the previous leader and those associated with them to hinder the work by the previous leader I served and those associated with them, we remained steadfast in the work that God has specifically assigned to us. As the leader in the church, I decided to choose honor. My final decision was to sanctify that leader in the eyes of the people. I took the same stance as David in 1 Samuel 24:9–12 (HCSB):

> [9] David said to Saul, "Why do you listen to the words of people who say, 'Look, David intends to harm you'?
>
> [10] You can see with your own eyes that the LORD handed you over to me today in the cave. Someone advised me to kill you, but I took pity on you

and said: I won't lift my hand against my lord, since he is the LORD's anointed.

[11] See, my father! Look at the corner of your robe in my hand, for I cut it off, but I didn't kill you. Look and recognize that there is no evil or rebellion in me. I have not sinned against you even though you are hunting me down to take my life.

[12] "May the Lord judge between you and me, and may the LORD take vengeance on you for me, but my hand will never be against you."

God will bless you when you take the high road. My response was only prayer. It was a priority to undergird the work with the only thing that would ensure its success and sustain it. As a leader, I maintained that posture. The church followed suit relentlessly as I built with those who were assigned to me. Our ministry was able to accomplish so many priority tasks in record time while executing tasks as would larger ministries. It was an amazing sight to behold. As a synchronized unit, we realized that rerouting our responses is an art form because it takes practice and grace. We must recognize that our human nature tends toward negativity unless we consciously choose to keep ourselves above it. It's like fishing. They throw out the fishing line with negativity bait on a hook. Will you be the fish who isn't aware and bites, thus taking the bait and ending up in a tug of war? Or will you be the wise fish who sees the bait and keeps on swimming past it?

Be vigilant and see it coming! You know what negativity looks and sounds like. So be present and aware for when it crosses your path. If you see it coming (like a baited hook dangling in the water!), you have a chance to stand back and breathe before biting! You can instead make a conscious choice not to engage with that negativity.

Remember, it is Not About You! Always remind yourself that another person's negativity is not about you. It is a reflection of something that is going on inside their mind and emotional system, and it is being projected around you or toward you. Too often we get tangled up in other people's negativity because our egos take it personally and react to their behavior or words. Rather — keep the accurate perspective that the person being negative is just a fellow human being who is in pain. It's not about you.

Chapter 5
Letting God Establish You Through Undisputed Evidence

Vindication is something we all desire, because injustices are committed toward us in this life.

Have you ever been falsely accused? Been the subject of gossip? Had lies spread about you? When you know deep in your heart that you are innocent, it is incredibly painful to hear rumors about yourself, to have your integrity brought into question, your reputation slandered. Some days, it is all you can do to get out of bed in the morning when you know the battle you face.

Some days, you simply cry out to God, "Vindicate me, oh God!"

Vindicate. Clear my name of false accusations. Prove my innocence through the truth. Present evidence justifying my actions. Defend me!

You have probably been there before. I know I have. And I am walking this path again, hearing my name slandered. I find myself begging God to vindicate me, to make my righteousness shine like the dawn and the justice of my cause like the noonday sun (Psalm 37:6).

How do we respond to these lies? How do we escape this vicious cycle of attack? How do we survive an evil attack against our name and our reputation?

Unjust attacks seem to be the common experience of humanity. A quick search of scripture finds many instances of the words "vindicate me," words typically cried out in the anguish of heart that comes with unjust attacks.

God has promised to protect us from harm. Yes, we may face false accusations on this earth. We may deal with unjust attacks. We may feel as if we are going to drown, as if our lives are over. But the truth is found in scripture: He is our Defender, our protection. The waves of slander may rock us and toss us all about, but He will not let them drown us. As long as we cling to Him for our protection, we will not be moved.

Founding a ministry had been one of the most daunting tasks I have undertaken to date. God called me to something that was bigger than I and what I assumed was outside of my skill set. Upon transitioning from a former place of ministry and enduring all that I had faced, the last thing in my mind was to pastor. I told God that I had done enough and that I was content in Him altering my life plan to anything, except dealing with His people and His church. Then again, He would answer that prayer by making me embrace what I was called to do. As much as I wanted to run, God would not allow it.

When I was getting ready to birth my ministry, it was a violent season in my life. As a result of my courage to transition, there was an all-out push to discredit and dismantle any endeavor I was undertaking. For over a year and a half, I developed and built a ministry in secret. All the while taking every hit and experiencing everything you could possibly think of being thrown at me by the former leader. It was a "witch hunt": attempts to find out everything I was doing or attempting to do and successfully cause interference. The goal was to kill it before it even had a chance to manifest. In my entire life, I have never experienced a leader feeling so threatened that they would result to acting like this. Then again, considering that individual and their true nature, it was expected.

I have this personal saying, "If you want to see how people really feel about you, start a church." You see how people you have collaborated with, assisted, and aided in ministry begin to shift. This shift is not for the better, either. God has his own way of bringing you into a place of enlightenment and awareness. He will not allow anything from the past to taint the future. God initiates a shift in the middle of the sift. When you sift flour, you help promote consistency in the ingredients by removing the larger particles that could result in densely textured baked goods or even ones that would sink in the middle. What God is getting ready to make of you in life requires you to be sifted so that you and your efforts do not sink. You have got to reach the resolve in your humanity that if God sifted me, he is getting ready to shift me!

Prior to founding the church, I went through a season where God literally showed me "who" was who. He revealed their intent, their purpose, and their aim. I came away from that experience knowing who was for me and who was clearly against me. Their insecurities, silent jealousy, and resentment began to openly manifest in a very public way. I became a target and competition. I was shocked at some of the things people did that they thought I did not even know about. God gave me the sobering clarity I needed to move forward. The enemy of your purpose does not care who he uses as a pawn to kill what you are becoming. He will use anyone. Some people are aware and willing while others are simply victims of their own naïveté. God's greatest gift to me in this place of sifting was sobriety. He knew that sobriety would be a necessity for my next place. It was in this place that I learned that the people I thought I needed were not necessary. Nor would they be a "fit" for the future. There are individuals who knew the "what" behind the "why," yet they still second-guessed my character. The people whom you both sacrificed for and served will sell you out, even under a false pretense, to prove their unwavering loyalty to a cause rooted in a leader's imbedded, deep-seated insecurities.

Proverbs 17:17 (KJV) says, "A friend loveth at all times, and a brother is born for adversity." Not everyone who started with me was there when the vision manifested. Adversity shows you who people really are. In my transition, there were definitely "tree-shaking eliminations" when it came to my connections, friendships, and dealings with people. Most people think I had a huge backing. The truth is that I did not. I did not have all of the bells and whistles. I started at ground zero. What I did have is a covering that believed in the God in me, the calling on my life and my divine assignment. I had an extremely small core that believed the same.

Finally, I made it to the moment where I was ready to present what God had given me to the authority that covered me. Although I was winded, weathered, and partially wounded, I believed in what God had spoken to me in secret and the vision I had received for ministry. As a result of a thorough meeting and discerning of intent, I received authorization to plant the ministry. This was an exciting moment in my life. However, I knew it would be an extreme fight to reach a place of fruition. I walked away from the meeting believing I had a solid team.

We had entered into the defining moment, received approval, were legitimately sanctioned, and passed the test. However, that was not good enough in their eyes. That individual's heart was not there. You could really tell it by the body language that was exhibited in the room. The most hurtful part, for me, was actually having a person on your team who was really not on your team. I would not find out the depth of it all until later in the future. The reason they articulated for withdrawing was ultimately a lie. To this day, they are doing the opposite of what they had articulated.

They were still battling their own trauma concerning the former situation. There was no interest and it was obvious. There was no investment. I do not fault them. However, an honest conversation would have been appreciated and adjustments made beforehand. I could have accepted a straightforward "no" instead of posing as a team member. That conversation never happened though. I and the two other members of the team were "ghosted." No explanations were received either. Many efforts were made to reach out, but it was to no avail. After so many rejections, uninterested engagements, and being ignored, I had to simply note it and move on. We moved forward. We did not miss a beat.

We would later find out that I was unintentionally compromised by that same team member whom we trusted following the meeting. It would later be revealed to me in casual conversation that the person leaked information about our potential next moves as a team. It was here I learned, "Sometimes, it's your friends who keep your enemies updated about you. Be careful." I am glad that this person did not remain a part of the team. Never question whom God removes from your life. After all, He hears their conversations when you are not around. He knows their true intentions and feelings toward you. I am of the belief that you do not watch what people say, but you watch what they do. The common trend was that they aligned with the very same people that we had disconnected from for good reason. It all clearly played out. They ended up being wielded by a person who was connected to the former. The distancing was obvious at this point. People enact "distancing" people because they cannot take the scrutiny of being associated with you in conflict or the process of development. Although this person did not have the courage to openly say this, it was easily discerned by the course consecutive actions that were actively demonstrated. As I contemplate it all, I saw it for what it was, simply resolved it, and let it go.

I birthed a ministry in a city 32 miles away from my hometown. Honestly, I always figured I would pastor in my hometown, yet God did not allow that to manifest. The beginnings of the ministry were small, intimate, and rooted in community. We revealed our approval in February before Convocation to what soon would become our congregation. After Convocation, we began ministry full throttle. We knew after being announced publicly that my former ministry was not excited about it. My former leader was furious. Because of limited information they were given, they set in motion the plan to cause an upset. The plot thickened. As a newly announced pastor, I knew I was in for quite the fight: a fierce one at that.

The difficult space would be the arduous road to launch service and subsequent pastoral installation. It is one that proved to be challenging. We the leadership, in full transparency, fully informed our new congregation of what we would be facing together. I did not hold anything back but expressed it with tact and decency. I imparted and taught the Biblical way to deal with adversity of this type. I supported and gave. March came, and the pandemic hit. However, it was an opportunity to shift. We were blessed to transition to a bigger space and afforded the opportunity to safely grow. As a new pastor, it was a blessing to be given an opportunity such as this. Moving into this new space was a direct manifestation of what I articulated to the people. During this time, we acquired so much. We hit the ground running and created community through social media groups, developing presence, and making impact.

All of a sudden, the oddest thing happened. I had members who suddenly stopped giving, attending, and even sowing because they were "turned off" of the ministry by the venomous sentiments that had been expressed through some of their mutual friends. The assumptions that they had developed were not even warranted. I was never antagonistic or beefing with the former pastoral leader who had an issue with my departure, contrary to what most thought. It was positioned that way and it was really absurd because I had said absolutely nothing at all since my departure. However, when I was continuously preached about over pulpits, everything I said, wrote, or posted became something to talk about and drew attention. It also drew speculation. As a pastor, this was not easy to endure as I had to hear the fabricated rationales from members through my staff regarding the people who disconnected. In retrospect, the sad part was explaining to them, with full transparency, the barriers we were up against, before we launched, seeing them fed this toxicity and being easily dissuaded by narratives that were created, and then watching them walk away. The gut-wrenching blow was them not even having the courage to have a closing conversation when I, as well as the entire leadership, had an open-door policy from the time we began. However, this did not stop us as many thought it would. Those who remained were faithful tithers and committed to the vision. Complete strangers were writing checks after viewing our ministry.

We accomplished so much. We secured our facility partnership, organ/Leslie, digital sound mixers, speakers, production equipment, sanitation stations, fog-steaming equipment, cordless microphones, stage lighting, podium, and all the other amenities for full-scale worship. We purchased it and owed no balances, etc. We experienced the favor of God in a tremendous way. Those who remained saw the faithfulness of God. Those who left simply watched from the outside. Your conscience will kill you every single time. For those people, it was the same feeling Peter had after he denied Jesus three times in public. To this day, their conviction causes them to remain in that same place and at a distance. Little do they know: our hearts are always open to receive them again and our posture of love for the long haul has not changed.

The road to my official pastor's installation would prove be a "trying stretch" for me as a leader. With the benefit of hindsight, it was the final stretch in getting to the other side of the most excruciatingly painful periods in the development of my call to pastoral ministry. Many people thought the ministry was going to die. A lot of people were banking on it. There was a prevailing "wait and see" disposition from most. I was always taught that support was never silent. God taught me to be consistent in work, even if no one is clapping. Applause is deceptive. Everyone clapping is not happy about your success or achievement. Some of the stuff that came out of certain people's mouths during this time was purely venomous.

People who are intimidated by you will talk badly about you in hopes others do not find you so appealing.

After all of the narratives put out in the city concerning me, the last thing my former leader wanted for my pastoral ministry was legitimacy. This is the reason there was such an effort to kill the ministry. It was hoped that the people connected to the ministry would lose faith in the vision and walk away and that I would simply give up. If I was legitimate, the discrediting and smearing campaign would be a moot point. However, that did not stop the leader from making every attempt possible to stop it from being a reality. Despite this leader's efforts, God's calling for me to was greater than anything that I was facing at their hands. I simply kept going. I tuned out the negativity and encouraged my people to do the same.

When we released our official installation announcement, excitement was in the air. It signaled the beginning of a shift. It was brought to our attention that people thought we were "gaslighting" the event by putting the homilist on the flyer. The former leader was using other people to run reconnaissance. This is the normal strategy that is used when they want to find out any information about anyone or anything that is going on with a person or group. Calls were made around the city and abroad to see if it was really happening, who was going and whether they were actually going to be participating in the service. Of course, the leader I formerly served was infuriated because they could not interfere with what

God was doing concerning myself or the ministry.

However, the depth of this leader's disrespect and dishonor had no limits. It was the norm of their nature to be this way. The leader, along with some of the congregation, had planned to come to the service. I was informed of their planned attendance. I was not so easily fooled by the sentiments that were expressed concerning their potential attendance. The leader's presence at this event carried an extreme, ulterior motive. Again, unbeknownst to my covering, this was a power flex and an attempt at outright intimidation. As a leader, I had already prepared for this type of action. I had seen this type of behavior, exhibited by this leader, played out in other people's installation services, particularly those who had left the ministry prior to my departure and started churches. To be truthful, I would have found this leader's presence to be highly disrespectful.

I want to express my feelings clearly concerning this matter. The installation was an official service. We had required all participants to register and for all special guests to confirm their attendance. There were safety protocols in place and there was only a limited number of seats. We received none of that information directly from that leader or the group that was planning to come to the service. They sought the work-around, which was really offensive. Any hosting leader would find it to be as such. This factor, in particular, literally left me boggled at the audacity and the nerve of this individual. The leader's intents were extremely distasteful.

The question in the back of my mind was this: How are you going to try to come to another ministry's event, particularly an official service of this nature, and not inform the host or leadership team in a direct manner? Common courtesy is to directly contact the leader or staff. Furthermore, why would you come to the official installation services of a pastor whose ministry you continuously attempted to kill? It did not make any sense to me at all. I was briefed of their potential attendance. I did not necessarily agree with what was being attempted, but I had to demonstrate maturity and discipline in my stance. I ensured that our leadership and teams were prepared. I put the appropriate accommodations in place. I knew it was highly likely that the leader and their guest would be present, but their pride would not let them. Their ego could not have endured it. Honestly, sitting through a service for the one you tried your best to eliminate would be unnerving to say the least.

Immediately after being briefed of their potential attendance, I went into prayer. I knew what this occasion meant for our ministry more so than for myself. I knew what the enemy was trying to do in a very public way. It was an intentional act of taunting. The spirit of intimidation was trying to rear its head. One of the tactics is to remain anonymous and to appear as innocent as possible. The job function of the spirit of fear and intimidation is to emotionally and spiritually paralyze so that the work will cease. I was not going to allow the enemy to attempt to bind us that way. There comes a time when you have to take a stand and that is exactly what I did.

I went into strategic prayer. I prayed all night. I laid it bare to God that night and expressed everything that I felt. My petition was selfless because I considered how others may receive or be affected by their presence, especially considering their knowledge of every single thing that had occurred to date. I awoke the next morning ready to face the day. I took on resilience and put trust in God. I believed Him to do what is right and that we would be fully prepared for anything we might face that day. The leader and those individuals who had planned to attend did not show up. I am a witness that God will not allow the past to taint your future. All signs pointed to Him teaching me that no matter what the threat may be, His hand will come against every single plan and plot of the adversary.

Forging Forward in Faith

Ministry leaders, yes, I said it, we often use the notion that good outweighs the bad to justify remaining connected to a place or a person that we are not yet ready to let go physically, emotionally and mentally. Many of us cannot move past our memories. Yes, there were good times, but there were also bad times. Those bad times were extremely costly and altered our lives. We hold on to our memories in false hopes that we will go back to when times were good. In forging my path forward, I want to share some wisdom with those who have boldly taken steps like me and chose never to turn back.

Here is my first admonishment: Do not re-open a toxic issue for the sake of closure.

In Philippians 3:13 (KJV), Paul says, "Brethren, I count not myself to have apprehended: but this one thing I do, forgetting those things which are behind, and reaching forth unto those things which are before…."

Closure means finality: letting go of what once was. Finding closure implies a complete acceptance of what has happened and an honoring of the transition away from what's finished to something new. In other words, closure describes the ability to go beyond imposed limitations in order to find different possibilities. Too many of us have fallen victim to the dysfunctional concept of what I call "the almost moment." You know, that person you were sort of working or collaborating with, and then, all of a sudden, they fall off the face of the earth with no explanation? You cannot necessarily call it a breakdown of connection because there were not any terms established. Plain and simple, you were "ghosted." If the other person cannot dignify you with an explanation as to why he or she no longer wants to be connected to you, then the reason is probably pathetic and superficial. That can happen in platonic friendships too, but no matter the case, you still need closure.

Even in exclusive, serious connections, shifts can happen without warning. Some of you have been both the victim and offender in both of these situations, so the term "closure" is quite familiar to you. In theory, closure is supposed to provide us cure-all. If we know what exactly went wrong and what we can improve upon, then we can close the door on that past issue and move on. Isn't that what we all want after a separation, break up, shift, or transition? To get over it and move on? To leave the baggage of the past behind us and move forward?

Closure is this abstract concept that we cannot see or feel, but we base our entire recovery on it. We theorize a million different reasons why things happened a certain way or why it just didn't work out. Most of the time, the real reason it didn't work out is probably something you are better off not hearing or even knowing. God knows what you do not know. That, in itself, is a great blessing! Because if you did, you would be trying to find ways to manipulate a fix that would only result in a messier outcome.

Closure can be mean; it can be nasty, hurtful and regressive. Your past will always be your past, and it is important to appreciate the past because it molds you into the person you are and the person you will become. But the past essentially doesn't exist anymore; all of your power and purpose is in this present moment and dragging problems from the past is only bringing you down. You didn't get closure? Guess what? It's time to move on. Let it go! Whatever it was, it did not work out. Accept the fact that it just was not meant to be, or the timing was off. Do you really want to reopen old wounds with pieces of closure you can obsess over for the next six to eight months of your life? If the hurtful situation or experience did not provide any closure, it is likely because you were spared from being hurt even more, or that situation was entirely too toxic to unravel for the sake of understanding and simply wasn't going to work, no matter what you did.

Let me "keep it 100" with you. Why would you want to be connected to inconsistency? You deserve respect, consistency, and commitment. Stop rereading every text to try to figure out what went wrong. Trust me, if someone walks away from you without a conversation, let them keep walking. You are better off without that critical level of instability. You do not need anyone in your life who is "unsure" about you. Stop stalking them on social media; it will only make things worse. Stop ruining every opportunity you have to interact with people in social settings articulating your hurt. Stop picking up unhealthy practices (smoking, drinking, sexing, and settling) because you are trying to fill a void and feel some type of retribution. You are never going to be able to have all the answers for why things did not work out. You must know that if it did not happen, it was because it was for a purpose. Most importantly, one that God will reveal as you move forward. Uncertainty is in every aspect of life, and you will be brought much more uncertainty in future times.

The key to grasping uncertainty is learning to live with the fact that you will not be able to figure everything out; all you can do is look at yourself, take everything you learned from the situation, and close the door behind you as you leave the past in the past. It is simple. Have faith in God. He absolutely has faith in you, even past all of the mistakes. And His love does not flinch at your flawed humanity. After all, that is what He sent his Son to die for. You have far better achievements, people, and experiences awaiting you. Obsessing over closure is only holding you back from unleashing your inner potential and the future God has for you.

Every person we meet or have a relationship of any kind with teaches us something about ourselves and about the world. Take that lesson with you and know that, although circumstances might be tough now, the lesson will serve its purpose in due time. Closure is not a need; it is something we think we need. If you cannot get closure, you are probably better off. Let it go, move forward and start the next chapter of your life with the lessons you have learned. Do not waste another moment of your life tormenting yourself with the toxic.

We need to exercise a degree of caution in the way we think about our past. We would not have done the things we used to do if they had not been attractive to us, and we need not think they could not become attractive again if we gave them the opportunity. We may have grown stronger, but we are not yet invincible. It would be impossible to forget completely the sins of our past. In fact, it would not be good to forget them — we need the memory of those things to keep us humble. But if we cannot keep certain memories from coming back, we can at least refuse to entertain them hospitably. We may have to look back for practical reasons now and then, but we dare not look back longingly.

It is a dangerous thing to replay the still-enjoyable aspects of the memory of things that tried to kill us physically, spiritually, mentally, and emotionally. Like Lot and his family who were told to leave Sodom and not look back, we need, in the case of some things, to leave them alone for the rest of our lives. We cannot afford to have any fine print in our contract with God. By His grace, we've been able to close certain doors. Re-opening them is … well, unthinkable.

Never lose sight of God's goodness. Nothing can cause us to doubt God's goodness more than affliction. But God can use your problem for eventual good, although you cannot see how. Affirm God's goodness, and constantly remind yourself of His unceasing love and care. Never give up. When the struggle wearies you to the point of giving up, give in to Christ and never to your circumstances. God promises to sustain you in your trials and either bring you through them or give you His all-sufficient grace to endure them. He will never fail or forsake you, and that is truth enough to persevere.

In the game of chess, there is a particular move called the "Unexpected Gambit!" This move is played frequently at high levels. It probably doesn't "feel right," because black moves the same pawn twice in the first three moves and offers to sacrifice that pawn the second time it moves forward. However, this move reveals the unexpected beauty and infinite variety of chess. The elements (time, space, and force) are always intermingled, and we often trade one for the other at many points in the game. When God is getting ready to make an unexpected move through transition, He uses Time, Space, and

Force. I went through a phase of asking God if there was any other way he could have positioned certain events in my life so that I could have avoided this painful transition— I mean, I kept asking every day. But I found my answer: if God orchestrated the way out it is because He has greater for you. Once I realized this, God responded, "Where you wanted to settle was too small." A lot of us want to settle in a small place called "satisfied." More often than not, we are satisfied with what is totally unacceptable. You cannot stay there! God will not allow you to settle for small when His grace is more than sufficient. Refuse to be a big fish in a small pond. Do not settle for the stream, pond or river when the ocean of possibility is infinite. God is getting ready to make an unexpected move!

Never forget that God always works behind the scenes on your behalf - God is for you and on your side. You can handle adversity because He can. Never take matters into your own hands. Wait on the Lord. An Encouragement: "Always remember you are braver than you believe, stronger than you seem, smarter than you think, and twice as beautiful as you had ever imagined!" Never deny the power of God's promise. God's Word contains promises just for your situation. God promises to vindicate you. And vindication will surely come. Do not take matters into your own hands. As Psalm 27:14 says, "Wait on the Lord; be of good courage, and he shall strengthen your heart. Wait, I say, on the LORD."

CONCLUSION

I wrote this book to tell the heart of what I experienced from an intimate level. The book is not a ploy to gain sympathy for what I faced as a servant leader. I am not a victim at all. I fully accept the fact that the pain was all a part of the journey to the completeness purpose. I can honestly attest that my evolution came through the resistance I faced and antagonistic agendas brought on by these experiences. My progress was not stopped by interference, either. This book is not an act of retribution or revenge in any shape, form or fashion. Experience is the best teacher. I desire for this to empower other ministry leaders to have the courage to transition and turn their pain into something extremely powerful for their next place in God. In the end, He does allow "all things to work together."

I want this book to be both a cautionary lesson and to shed light on what to look for in these types of situations, so other people do not subject themselves or connect their gifts to leaders who carry this type of nature or agenda. These types of circumstances are very much real and often go unnoticed by the mainstream or are swept under the rug. I wanted to turn my silent pain and process to recovery into a guidebook to help someone who may find themselves in this space, having to wrestle with embracing the call, protecting the ministry that is being birthed inside of them and then fighting to see it safely manifest. I want you to know what it really looks like in real time.

I also want you to realize that leaders or people who have participated in sabotage, plots, and conspiracies against others know what they did and the reasons why they did it. However, the truth would never surface because it would require honesty to admit that their course of actions carried ill intent, ulterior motives, and ill will. I want to stand in the gap and confront the warped idea of healing. This notion of "Get Healed" is often promoted by the perpetrators within these ministry social circles as part of their agenda to subtly bully folks into silence to just "get over it." The truth is that some of your colleagues, friends, and homies were the ones who violated, sabotaged, offended, transgressed, and wounded some of these people. And did so without any remorse, at that.

Pain has a point of view, but so does healing and wholeness. There are many people in the church who have suffered from public and private interference from leaders. These people have lived in years of pain and suffering and are trying to navigate through all of the unresolved spaces. Living under altered narratives placed on their character has caused shame as people's hearts were turned against them and doors of opportunity were closed to them. I know this has proven to be challenging on so many fronts. When faced with this, giving up often seems to be the easier option.

These men and women have been stigmatized, excluded, ostracized, and outcast. We allow people to live under stigma. Stigma taints and tarnishes. Silence is betrayal. Silence is endorsement. Silence is even consent. Many times, silence occurs because people choose loyalty and allegiance to a personality instead of the principle of doing "right" by people. Once the truth is revealed, we never seek to restore or right what has been said both in public and private. We allow people to get hurt. This has got to stop.

    These people who are wounded are not rebellious, self-seeking or have their own agenda. The issue is the insecurity of so many pastors and church leaders. In the church today, we tend to shy away from discussing not only this issue, but the reality of what this looks like from the anointed and gifted individuals who experience trauma from it. We continue to turn a blind eye to it while people suffer to piece together their mental states, make sense of their call, reconstruct their lives from the devastation caused by these types of leaders, and fearlessly forge forward to their future in faith. I believe it is critically important that we take responsibility in the kingdom for the public restoration of people who have undergone these types of situations.

Transitioning must be done with courage. However, healing after the transition requires that you have an honest confrontation with the pain that the situation caused and the disappointment that comes along with it. It takes a sincere acknowledgement. For ministry leaders who have endured strife-filled transitions, pain is often layered. They have not only fought for their recovery but have to reconstruct their lives at the same time. I want people to know that "Yes, you can heal without an apology."

However, you do not have to deny the truth of your healing and recovery process to make the people who hurt you feel comfortable either. I want the cycle to stop. I want ministry leaders and their gifts to flourish without going through unnecessary injury or spiritual wounding.

Too often, people remain silent in the church while others suffer things people have no idea about. Not everyone is mentally equipped to handle being tried in the court of public opinion, shamed, antagonized, damaged and the like. In fact, there are some that never fully recover at all. They end up walking away from God, His Church and His people. They commit suicide. We never talk about that. Other leaders, in the same environment in ministry, watch people suffer cruelty and say nothing. Insiders and outsiders make light of situations in jest, gossip, and perpetuate the cycles fueled by senseless activity. There is jeering at another person's calamity. They deflect from themselves by participating in order to "fit in" while struggling to remain connected to those who are attacking others. Another person's demise does not secure your come up. I want people in the Kingdom of God to actually recognize that notion. We need people to do the work of restoration, healing and setting things right.

    I have been silent for two years of my life. I was able to sit with the pain, anguish, and realities of every moment that came along with this transition. I had to walk out a journey as a person, pastor, and leader. However, this is the last step in wholeness for me. Penning my experience as a monument to my triumph was therapeutic and liberating. It is a sobering reminder that you can live through and come back from anything, especially when you have a God who is for you, people who love and genuinely support you and mental toughness to endure spiritual rehabilitation and recovery. Live on purpose. The wounds are what substantiate your win. Survive, thrive, and become!

A MOMENT OF TRANSITION

Terence George Craddock

(excerpt)

In all lives
where great character
is attained...
comes a moment
requiring
exceptional transition.

Sometimes
historically to achieve
something revolutionary...
profoundly better
something imminently bad
must transpire first.

TRANSITIONING WITHOUT FEAR: "NEED TO KNOWS" FOR THE NEXT PLACE!

Being made whole on the other side of healing makes you look at things from a different viewpoint. I have walked this path for two years. I have embraced every tear, every flashback, the bouts of severe anger, endured the excruciating hurt, faced the shame and the guilt, questioned if things could have been another way. However, all of it was necessary. Upon emerging from this transitional space, I resolved that I never wanted anyone to encounter the same situations that I did. I wanted them to know "what" to actually look for and to value themselves beyond remaining in a space that is not ideal for the growth of their purpose. I wanted to give them practical insight.

Toxic people in leadership and in general challenge logic. Some are idyllically ignorant of the negative impact that they have on those around them, and others seem to develop gratification from creating disorder and pushing other people's buttons. Either way, they create unnecessary complication, contention, and, worst of all, tension. Toxic people in leadership, as a servant leader, can drive you crazy because their behavior is so senseless. Make no mistake about it; their behavior truly goes against proper judgment.

So why do you let yourself to respond to them emotionally and get sucked into the muddled whirlwind? The more unreasonable and off-base someone is, the simpler it should be for you to disconnect yourself from their deceptions and set-up's. Quit trying to beat them at their own game. Distance yourself from them expressively and refuse interaction. You do not need to respond to the emotional chaos — only the facts. Maintaining emotional space requires awareness. You cannot stop someone from pressing your buttons if you do not recognize when it's happening. Sometimes you will find yourself in situations where you will need to regroup and choose the best way forward. This is fine, and you should not be afraid to buy yourself some time to do so.

If you are going to have to rectify or deal with a situation going future-forward, it is better to give yourself some time to plan the best way to go about it. I gave myself two years combined with professional therapy and it worked. Successful people know how important it is to live to fight another day, especially when your foe is a toxic individual. I thank God for sound counsel and wisdom of my covering, elders, and covenant connections who walked me through it and helped me see the future past a series of momentary discomforts. In conflict, unchecked emotion makes you "dig your heels in and fight" the kind of battle that can leave you severely damaged. When you read and respond to your emotions, you are able to choose your battles wisely and only stand your ground when the time is right. I know now more than ever that Ecclesiastes 3:1 (KJV) is true when it says, "To everything there is a season, and a time to every purpose under the heaven."

Assaulting another person, shifting blame, and passing judgment on another severely all come from the same place: the attacker's attempt to displace some of their own injurious feelings onto you. By putting the focus on to you, and what they think you did wrong, they can take the focus off of themselves, and their own deficiencies of character. But they can also put you in a one down position, promoting themselves to a position of power. And people who attempt to gain power this way — through belittling others — do so because they do not feel powerful in their own lives, and the only appeasement is to attempt to control others. People who hurt others to feel better about themselves, may not know how to feel good any other way, and may also have very insubstantial and archaic ego structures. What this means is that their awareness of self is immature and demarcated through their ability to control others. And what people who attack do not have control over is their own sense of self — because attacks come from unresolved information, an insensible need to recoup power, and are warranted by a professed feeling of being wronged or hurt somewhere in their lives.

Being personally attacked, accused, and condemned puts us all on the defensive, and we may want to throw our own daggers, yet attacking back simply suggests confrontation. And while you may feel as if it is wrong that you were harmed and want to rectify the behavior, it is never your job to correct anyone's behavior but your own. Instead, when someone goes on the offense after you, your focus needs to be on aligning boundaries to protect yourself. This is what is meant by empathic confrontation. Empathic confrontation essentially means recognizing that bad behavior comes from a place of pain and confusion, and then setting limits.

The power of my full recovery was found in my community. It was my community that reaffirmed my value. The objective of a person blaming, criticizing, or attacking you is to make you feel awful, and it usually does. Attacks hurt everyone, after all. So instead of defending yourself to the person attacking — which will only cause war — reaffirm your value to yourself. Use the attack to take a look at your life, do an honest assessment, and recognize the good things you do, and the value you bring. If you feel you could do better, make a plan to change what you think needs changing. And if you feel you are doing everything in your power to be the person you want to be, then remind yourself of that. But make it your choice to decide how you are doing and if you need to change — not anyone else's. After all, it's your life. Attacks, criticisms and accusations hurt, but they are also exampling of bad behavior. And while the invitation is always there to strike back, the opportunity is also there to use these things to strengthen your own good behavior, to not fall prey to the temptation to also behave badly, and to remind yourself of why being nice and integral matters.

So what can we do about personal attacks?

1. Do not lower yourself to their level. I know it is easier to say this than to do this. It is hard not to respond in kindness when you are under personal

attack. But getting into the gutter is almost always counterproductive and leads to escalation – not resolution. Instead, be professional and maintain your composure. You will lose if you lose it too.

2. Focus on your goal. Folks sometimes engage in personal attacks to distract or divert you from the real issues on the table. Perhaps they have weak leverage and the conversation was focused on their poor replacement. Or maybe they thought you would forget about your power, ability and influence if they came at you personally. Your response? Keep your goals and interests front and center. Written agendas can help here, too,

especially if you anticipated the attacks due to your counterpart's reputation.

3. Take a break. Do not underestimate the power of a cooling off period. You need time for their adrenaline surge to dissipate. Of course, you may want to take a day, week, month, or even longer.

4. In dealings with others, particularly in religious organizational settings or if your transition involves longstanding relationships, consider going over your attacker's head and requesting a new counterparty. This should not be a first resort, but sometimes the inherent risk of this move backfiring

(if your request is denied) is outweighed by the potential benefit of moving forward productively. At the least, this will hopefully bring some pressure on your counterpart to behave in a more professional way.

5. Exercise your leverage. At the end of the day, your ability to impact your counterpart's behavior may be mostly dependent upon your fundamental leverage — the value of your alternative (or a Plan B that is relative to your counterpart's alternative). The easier it is for you to walk away and the better your Plan B, the more difficult it is for your counterpart to interfere. The worse their Plan B, the higher the likelihood they will avoid

personal attacks. So if you have strong leverage, make a move toward your Plan B. Then closely monitor their reaction. In my own transition, I observed that the personal attacks of the leader tended to take one thing and twist it, or blow it out of proportion, to seem like that was all there is to me. Often, they are based on a half-truth or a distortion of what was said or did. They painted me as all bad rather than speaking the truth that was upheld by their own insecurities.

Sometimes, we just need to remind ourselves that everyone has the right to state their opinion. It does not mean they are correct — you get to choose whether or not you agree with them. Even the most hurtful attack loses its power when we realize this. This is the area where most people tend to sell themselves short. They feel like because they work, live, or are in ministry at a certain location with someone, they have no way to control the chaos. This could not be further from the truth. Even if you work with someone closely on a ministry team, that does not mean that you need to have the same level of one-on-one interaction with them that you have with other team members. You can establish a boundary, but you will have to do so consciously and proactively. If you set boundaries and decide when and where you will engage a difficult person, you can control much of the chaos. The only trick is to stick to your convictions and keep boundaries in place when the person tries to encroach upon them, which they always will either directly or through other people.

Where you center your attention decides your emotional state. When you are preoccupied with the problems you are facing, you create and prolong negative feelings and pressure. When you focus on actions to better yourself and your circumstances, you create a sense of personal usefulness that produces positive emotions and reduces stress. When it comes to toxic people, fixating on how outlandish and problematic they are results in giving them power over you. Quit thinking about how disquieting your difficult person is and focus instead on how you are going to go about handling them. This makes you more effective by putting you in control, and it will reduce the amount of stress you experience when counteracting anything they may try to throw at you.

Emotionally intelligent people are quick to forgive, but that does not mean that they forget. Forgiveness requires letting go of what has happened, so that you can move on. It does not mean you will give a wrongdoer another chance. Successful people are unwilling to be bogged down unnecessarily by others' mistakes, so they let them go quickly and are assertive in protecting themselves from future harm.

To answer the question that most want to know and already have heard various accounts about:

Yes, a specific religious institution and a leader tried to destroy everything about me, but I would not let it. I know now for sure that who I am in God. Most importantly, I know who I am as a person and that is far greater than some lascivious deviants' validation.

I saw people get ordained, affirmed, consecrated, elevated, licensed, appointed and such, and soon after I saw their life's purposes and ministries lowered into the ground and dirt thrown in their faces, unbeknownst to them. They were faithful, loyal, giving, and submitted in more ways than one, and at the end it cost them their lives and their purpose.

As someone who has suffered at the hands of the people "in the church," I still believe in the Church (institution) that Christ established and died for. However, there is nothing that can be offered to me to keep me from confronting its ills and the things that make people suffer while leading or sitting in the pews. People are dying unnecessarily and at the expense of fragile egos and small-minded people.

We oftentimes dismiss people based on what others say about them. But has it ever occurred to you that the person speaking ill just may be the perpetrator? People are rewarded for doing wrong. Leader's action towards people are "swept under the rug" or a blind eye is turned all because of who they appear to be, their stature and influence. This is not ok. However, there is another person, on the other side of all of it, whose life is wounded and now they are forced to navigate through discomfort and pick up the rubble while continually dealing with all collateral damage that comes as a result of being in these types of situations. There are leaders that teach people that if they stick by them that they will go places. They buy loyalty even if they have to pay for it with the blood of the innocent.

But even with all that is wrong, there are still so many loving leaders out there — that will not harm you. I managed to find that in my journey and it had led to me becoming the person I am today. The Church is successful, victorious — and yes, the church needs you, all of you — flaws and all.

My question to you is this:

If you leave, who will help restore and protect those like you? Believe me your story is needed, the good, the bad and the ugly.

Yes, shattered people cut me! And guess what? I healed.

Some of our wounds need sutures while others need bandages. For some it's just a paper cut and for others a laceration. Nonetheless we all needed mending — Heal so you can help!

www.ingramcontent.com/pod-product-compliance
Lightning Source LLC
Chambersburg PA
CBHW072131160426
43197CB00012B/2065